the light
of the mind

the
light
of
the
mind : st. augustine's
theory
of

knowledge

Ronald H. Nash

The University Press of Kentucky

Standard Book Number 8131-1175-7
Library of Congress Catalog Card Number 69-19765

COPYRIGHT © 1969 BY THE UNIVERSITY PRESS OF KENTUCKY

A statewide cooperative scholarly publishing agency serving Berea College,
Centre College of Kentucky, Eastern Kentucky University, Kentucky State
College, Morehead State University, Murray State University, University
of Kentucky, University of Louisville, and Western Kentucky University.
Editorial and Sales Offices: Lexington, Kentucky 40506

IN MEMORIAM

JOEL W. KOCAB

1936–1965

preface

St. Augustine is the bridge that links ancient philosophy and early Christian theology to the thought patterns of the Middle Ages. But the influence of Augustine's philosophy in general and his epistemology in particular extends far beyond medieval philosophy. Such modern philosophers as Descartes and Malebranche carry the stamp of Augustinism upon their philosophies. What is not so well known is that even some of the most original ideas of Berkeley and Kant can be found anticipated in Augustine.

In the light of the enduring significance of Augustine's philosophy it is odd that no study in English devoted exclusively to an examination of his theory of knowledge has appeared. But the *raison d'être* for this book goes beyond my desire to remove this lacuna in Augustinian studies. I have attempted to offer an interpretation of Augustine's doctrine of illumination that is significantly different from the ones proposed by scholars who belong to the Thomist tradition. In dealing with the history of philosophy, one must mention the names of Etienne Gilson and Frederick Copleston with the greatest respect. However, I am forced to differ with these men (and others, such as Vernon J. Bourke) regarding their understanding of Augustine's illumination theory. Not only do their interpretations tend to obscure what I regard as the real Augustinian position, but they ignore what may have been Augustine's greatest contribution to the history of phi-

losophy, a theory of knowledge that on several important points anticipates Immanuel Kant.

However, before it can join the debate, this book first will have to clarify the relationships that exist among the many aspects of St. Augustine's theory of knowledge. His views on skepticism and truth, on faith and reason, and on sense perception, cogitation, and intellection will require study. The most significant topics, however, are his doctrines of divine illumination and intellection. Augustine makes it clear that man can know this present temporal, corporeal world only because he first knows the eternal, incorporeal, intelligible world of ideas that exists in the mind of God. This view seems to commit Augustine to the position that unless he can explain intellection (man's knowledge of eternal and unchangeable truth), he will be unable to explain how man knows anything. Intellection and illumination are the areas in which most of the current debate of Augustine's theory of knowledge is occurring.

Through the years many contributed directly or indirectly to this study. They include Professors Carlton Gregory and Terrelle B. Crum of Barrington College, Professor Roderick Chisholm of Brown University, Professor Richard Taylor of the University of Rochester, Dr. John L. Benson of Denver, Colorado, and Professor Theodore Denise of Syracuse University. Professors Gordon Clark (Butler University), Sheldon Peterfreund (Syracuse), Panyot Butchvarov (Iowa), and my colleague Professor John Stahl read the manuscript and offered many helpful comments and criticisms. A special word of acknowledgment must go to the late Milton Williams, former professor of philosophy at Syracuse University, whose character and teaching continue to be an inspiration to those who knew him.

Chapter One first appeared as an article in the Fall 1964 issue of *The Gordon Review*. Portions of chapters

five and six were first published in the article "St. Augustine on Man's Knowledge of the Forms," which appeared in the Spring 1967 issue of *The New Scholasticism*. I am grateful to the editors of both journals for their permission to use the material in this book.

R. H. N.

contents

chapter
        one : the structure
            of st. augustine's
            theory of
            knowledge

A<small>NY</small> attempt to study St. Augustine's theory of
knowledge is confronted immediately by three difficulties.
First of all, even to talk about Augustine's philosophy as
philosophy in a sense does an injustice to his thought.
While philosophy and theology can easily be distinguished
in the writings of a philosopher such as St. Thomas
Aquinas, one finds no such bifurcation in Augustine.
Augustine believes that the true philosophy is also the
true theology. Faith and reason are not psychologically
separate activities that may be exercised independently.
Augustine phrased this truth as I believe in order that I
may know. Faith and reason both are necessary elements
of knowledge. Thus, any attempt to isolate the philosophy
of St. Augustine from the corpus of his writings seems to
force his thought into a framework foreign to the heart
and spirit of Augustine. But despite this difficulty,
Augustine's philosophy must be studied. In such a study,
however, one must ask—to use Copleston's words—"What
ideas of Augustine are philosophical in the academic understanding of the term."[1]
    The second difficulty is the frequent vagueness in

Augustine's thought. His writings lack the systematization and completeness often demanded of philosophers. Etienne Gilson notes that many who delve into the Augustinian doctrine

> often regret the unfinished quality of most of its fundamental positions. Perhaps with a little more practice these philosophers will come to realize that they complain of a characteristic proper to the doctrine itself, for this incompleteness is no less a part of it than the digressive method for which it is criticized. We immediately try to find a system in these writings, i.e., a collection of truths ready-made and linked together in an order that helps us to understand and remember them. What they give us is a method, i.e., the proper order to follow in a long series of efforts which we must make ourselves.[2]

Whitney J. Oates makes a similar point in suggesting that Augustine's philosophy is an "open" as opposed to a "closed" system. As Oates explains these distinctions, a closed philosophical system, such as that found in the writings of Aristotle and Aquinas, produces interpreters who are more content to explain the thought of their master than to advance philosophical inquiry. In contrast an open philosophical system, such as Plato's, is one "which comprehends within it all aspects of reality, one which admits the fact that human speculation on ultimate questions is always in process, and cannot in any final sense ever be completed. It is 'germinal' and at the same time peculiarly vulnerable to strict rational attack."[3]

It was not Plato's intention, Oates contends, to give the world a system of philosophy. This is suggested by Plato's form of writing. *The Dialogues* are a perfect vehicle to keep philosophical inquiry moving and to keep it from jelling into a system of dogmas. Plato also suggests this when he has Socrates say that things put into writing, in some sense die, while the spoken words of men, their

personal communication, live on.[4] Oates concludes that Augustine's philosophy is just such an open system. Thus, we should not be discouraged by what seems to be vagueness and incompleteness. Rather, we should be encouraged to take upon ourselves, as each generation of Augustine's students has done, the task of applying his insights and suggestions to the problems of our own day.

One further difficulty is especially relevant to this study. It was never Augustine's plan to construct a systematic theory of knowledge. Throughout his writings he insists that knowledge is not to be sought for its own sake; instead, man should seek knowledge so that through it he may attain true happiness. Augustine's view is not so much that knowledge will make the attainment of happiness easier but that the knowledge of absolute truth is a necessary condition for happiness. Although Augustine's practical interest in knowledge keeps him from giving us the kind of systematic discussion of certain topics that one finds in Hume or Kant, there is nonetheless a certain benefit that follows. The fact that knowledge is related to God and to the human quest for happiness insures the importance of epistemology for Augustine.

It must not be inferred that no order or system is to be found in Augustine's discussion of epistemological topics. It would be wrong to think that Augustine's writings contain only occasional, piecemeal, confused, or inconsistent remarks about such matters as faith, reason, truth, sensation, and knowledge. On the contrary, one can find throughout his writings the same general framework of knowledge. From some of his earliest letters[5] to the definitive writings of his mature years[6] he accepted approximately the same position.

Augustine came to Christianity by way of Neoplatonism. His reading of the Neoplatonists helped answer the problems and remove the obstacles that Manicheanism and skepticism had placed in the way of his becoming a Chris-

tian. Thus, many of the distinctive elements of Augustine's philosophy were formulated consciously or unconsciously under the influence of Plotinus. Many affinities exist between Augustine and Plotinus on such matters as illumination, the relationship between soul and body, the arguments for the immortality of the soul, sensation, and the solution of the problem of evil. Augustine's fidelity to the Christian Scriptures and his own genius produced major alterations in the Plotinian doctrine, but Plotinus' influence cannot be ignored. In fact, many elements of Augustine's thought can be understood only when they are seen in the light of the Platonic tradition in philosophy.

The influence of Plotinus—and through him the influence of Plato—is evident in the pattern of Augustine's theory of knowledge. Plotinus held that there were orders or levels of reality and that this order was always a descent from The One.[7] All reality is derived from The One. The One produces by emanation the level of intelligence (*nous*), which in turn produces the level of soul that is manifested in the structure of the world. Corresponding to Plotinus' downward way of becoming was his upward way of salvation. Man's ultimate goal should be union with The One, but in order to attain this union, the soul must rise upward—it must free itself from its bondage to the body, pleasure, and sensation. As the soul leaves behind the realm of sensation, it comes closer to its ultimate goal, The One. This view was derived from Plato.

For Plato the ontological course proceeds downward from the form of the good to the eternal and unchangeable forms and finally to the world of particulars. The epistemological path rises upward. Man finds himself tied by his body to the world of sensible particulars. As Plato's allegory of the cave shows so well,[8] the path of knowledge leads upward. As man frees himself from the domination of the senses, he climbs the scale of knowledge. Leaving

behind the realm of opinion, he turns to the realm of the forms and there finds knowledge.

Augustine makes similar remarks about the relationship between ontology and epistemology. Augustine's ontology consists of an hierarchical structure of reality with God, its creator, at the apex and the world of bodies at the lowest level. His epistemology finds man beginning with sensation but attempting to climb by way of reason to the eternal ideas in the mind of God.[9] Augustine conceived of God as both the source of human existence and the goal of human knowledge.

The following schema shows the important elements of Augustine's structure of thought and the relationships existing among them:

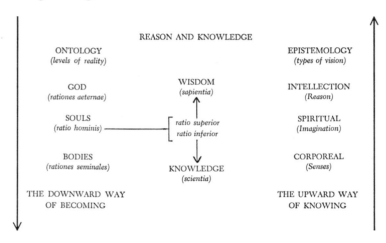

REASON AND KNOWLEDGE

ONTOLOGY (levels of reality)		EPISTEMOLOGY (types of vision)
	WISDOM (sapientia)	
GOD (rationes aeternae)		INTELLECTION (Reason)
SOULS (ratio hominis)	ratio superior / ratio inferior	SPIRITUAL (Imagination)
BODIES (rationes seminales)	KNOWLEDGE (scientia)	CORPOREAL (Senses)
THE DOWNWARD WAY OF BECOMING		THE UPWARD WAY OF KNOWING

Augustine in good Platonic fashion links ontology and epistemology. There is a similarity between the structure of being and the structure of knowing. It must be shown first that this schema faithfully represents the structure of Augustine's thinking on epistemology. Also, it is necessary to make some preliminary explanations of the terms used and the relationships that exist among the various notions.

Augustine's God is not the finite demiurge of Plato nor the transcendent One of Plotinus. He is the triune God of the Christian Scriptures who created *ex nihilo* all of reality.[10] Augustine's God is the "most high, most excellent, most potent, most omnipotent; most merciful and most just; most hidden and most near; most beauteous and most strong, stable, yet contained of none; unchangeable, yet bringing old age upon the proud and they know it not; always working, yet ever at rest; gathering, yet needing nothing; sustaining, pervading, and protecting; creating, nourishing, and developing; seeking and yet possessing all things."[11] God, who is immutable in both time and space, created the world of souls and bodies. Though the soul of man is mutable only in time and not in space, bodies are mutable in both time and space.[12]

Corresponding to each of these three levels of reality is a principle or *ratio*.[13] On the lowest level, the level of bodies, Augustine speaks of the *rationes seminales,* seed-like principles that exist in the nature of the world's elements. When God created the world, He embedded in the creation principles that guide its development.

On the highest level of reality, the level of God, Augustine finds the *rationes aeternae,* his equivalent of the Platonic forms. He describes the *rationes aeternae* as "principal forms or stable and unchangeable essences of things. They are themselves not formed, and they are eternal and always in the same state because they are contained in God's intelligence. They neither come into being nor do they pass away, but everything that can or does come into being and pass away is formed in accordance with them."[14] This important passage makes several significant points about the forms: (1) they are eternal and immutable; (2) they are the patterns of particular things; and (3) they are grounded in the mind of God. The last two points are especially important.

The forms or divine ideas are archetypal forms of created

reality. Like Plato, Augustine argues that before an architect builds an edifice, he must first have a model of what he intends to build. Similarly, God had a plan before He created the universe. His creation is patterned or copied after the divine ideas. Therefore, because the divine forms are the exemplary cause of everything that exists, they are the basic foundation of all created reality. Moreover, because the judgments men make must accord with the eternal forms, they are an indispensable element in human knowledge.

Augustine's point about the ontological status of the *rationes aeternae* was an important contribution to philosophic thought. Although Plato apparently taught that the forms and the demiurge were independent of each other, Augustine follows the lead of Philo[15] and Plotinus[16] and grounds the ideas in the mind of God.[17] This helps to explain certain characteristics of the *rationes*. Since they subsist in God's intellect, they share God's essential attributes and thus are eternal, necessary and unchangeable.

Augustine also speaks of the *ratio hominis*, the rational soul of man. He distinguishes two functions of man's reason. Man, existing as he does on the second level of reality, can look up toward eternal reality by means of the *ratio superior* (the higher reason), or he can look down upon corporeal, visible reality by means of the *ratio inferior* (the lower reason).[18] Augustine understands the higher and lower reasons to be not two separate faculties but simply two different functions of the same mind.[19] To his Platonically oriented mind it was inconceivable that the same function of man's mind could know both mutable and immutable reality.

The two functions of reason differ not only in their object but also in their result. In fact, so disparate were the results that Augustine distinguished two kinds of knowledge. The knowledge acquired through the *ratio superior* he called wisdom (*sapientia*), and that acquired

through the lower reason was called science or knowledge (*scientia*). Wisdom and knowledge differ in many respects. While science is a knowledge of true things, *i.e.*, a rational cognizance of the temporal, wisdom is a knowledge of truth, *i.e.*, an intellectual cognizance of the eternal.[20] Error is possible in *scientia* but not in *sapientia*. *Scientia* uses the method of investigation, but wisdom uses intuition. *Scientia* has as its object the temporal and mutable, and *sapientia* is knowledge of the eternal and immutable. Finally, the two kinds of knowledge differ according to their ends. The end of *scientia* is action or accomplishment. *Scientia* enables man to harvest better crops, construct better buildings, or wage war more effectively. Augustine's point still has force in our own day. Men do not seek to extend the frontiers of human knowledge so that they may then sit back and contemplate the wonders of the universe or worship its creator. *Scientia* is primarily sought because the lack of knowledge frustrates our efforts to do one thing or another, for example, cure cancer, provide new sources of energy, or travel to the moon. On the other hand, the end of *sapientia* is contemplation.[21] Augustine was always concerned with the pragmatic importance of knowing. As he put it, "Man has no reason to philosophize except with a view to happiness."[22] The contemplative life is superior to the active life.[23] However, this statement is not necessarily a plea for monasticism or retirement from the world. Wisdom is superior in the sense that it is concerned with the acquisition of happiness and the ultimate goal of human existence.[24] As man turns toward the eternal and unchangeable, he submits himself to a power beyond himself and finds satisfaction in contemplation. This is because the ultimate goal of wisdom is godliness, the worship of God, which alone can bring true blessedness.[25] But this does not make *scientia* worthless or unimportant; the preservation and sustaining of human life depends upon *scientia*. A knowledge of sensible

things is indispensable to practical living.[26] The superiority
of wisdom over science is simply the superiority that an
end or goal has over a means to that end. The activity of
scientia helps to make *sapientia* possible.

Augustine teaches that man can see three classes of
objects.[27] First, man can see physical objects, such as trees,
houses, and human bodies, which he can perceive through
his senses. Second, man can see representations of physical
things, for example, the picture in his mind formed by
memory or imagination. Finally, man can know non-
corporeal objects that cannot possibly be represented in
a corporeal way. This last class includes the *rationes
aeternae*.

Augustine distinguishes three levels of perception[28]
corresponding to the three types of objects that man can
know. The lowest level, sensation, is common to both
man and the brutes; the highest level, intellection, is
unique to man. This level is related to *sapientia*, since it
is the contemplation of eternal truths by the mind. Between the levels of intellection and sensation is another
domain that, like intellection, is peculiar to man.[29] It is
akin to *scientia*, the judgment of sense objects by rational
and eternal standards. Because man possesses reason and
brutes do not, man can have a rational knowledge of
sensible things: he can make rational judgments about
them and regard them as exemplifications of the eternal
forms. On this middle level, which Augustine calls cogitation (*cogitatio*),[30] man judges sensible things according to
the unchanging standards of the divine ideas. Because
reason plays a vital role on this level, it is unique to man,
but because it is a knowledge of sensibles and thus involves
a use of the various senses, it is a lower level of knowledge
than intellection.

A similar theory is advanced in the twelfth book of *De
Genesi ad Litteram*, where Augustine distinguishes three
types of vision. The lowest is corporeal vision.[31] This

includes perception through the bodily senses. Above this is what Augustine calls spiritual vision. He defines *spiritus* as a power or faculty of the soul in which the mind expresses images of corporeal things.[32] Spiritual vision is similar to cogitation in that it is a relating of the powers of the mind to the images of sensible things. Finally, Augustine mentions intellectual vision.[33] Through this vision man attains knowledge of God, the soul of man, virtues, and other universals, and this vision alone can produce *sapientia*. Augustine offers an example and asks his readers to consider the words of Jesus, "Love thy neighbor as thyself." The letters on the page are seen by corporeal vision; when our neighbor is absent, he can be seen only by spiritual vision; and love, which of course cannot be imaged, can be seen only through intellectual vision.[34]

Augustine comments on the relationship between corporeal and spiritual vision in *De Trinitate*.[35] He states that there are four steps in the transition from sensation to rational knowledge, or as he puts it in this context, from the bodily species (or form) to the species in the intuition. First, there is (1) the corporeal species, which is simply the external object as it is in itself. The corporeal species produces (2) the sensible species, which is the way the object appears for the sense organ. The sensible form causes a form in the mind that accounts for our present perception of the object. This is (3) the first form of the mental species. Finally, this latter form or image produces the image in the memory, which is (4) the form we actually perceive when we remember. Augustine admits that usually no distinction is made between the first two and the last two species. From these four species or forms he suggests that two kinds of vision result. "For there are two kinds of vision, the one of (sensuous) reception (*sentientis*), the other of conception (*cogitantis*). But in order that the vision of conception

may come to be, there is wrought for the purpose, in the memory, from the vision of (sensuous) perception something like it, to which the eye of the mind may turn itself in conceiving, as the glance of the eyes turns itself in (sensuously) perceiving to the bodily object."[36]

The passage does not mention intellectual vision, because it is only concerned with the two levels of perception related to sensation. The passage teaches that corporeal vision (or *sentientis*) occurs when the sensible object (the corporeal species) "informs" the sense organ. Spiritual vision occurs when the species of the memory forms thought.

The upward path of knowledge for Augustine involves the passage from sensation to the rational cognizance of temporal things (*scientia*) to the intellectual cognizance of eternal reality (*sapientia*). In spite of the vagueness and indefiniteness that can be found in much of Augustine's writings, the careful student can find in his work a general framework of thought that becomes evident in his earliest writings and apparently is accepted throughout his life.

chapter
two : on skepticism
and truth

Aₗₜₕₒᵤₒₕ the conjoining of skepticism and truth
may at first seem strange, they do—at least in Augustine's
philosophy—go together. If one rejects skepticism, as
Augustine did, then he must believe that truth exists and
that man can know it.

Augustine's attack on skepticism is a convenient start-
ing point for a study of his theory of knowledge. Logically,
the question "Can man know truth?" is prior to investigations into the subject of how man knows truth. If the
answer to the first question is negative, then there is
nothing left to study.

Augustine's interest in refuting skepticism was more
practical than theoretical. He believed that the question
of skepticism concerned life, morality, and our souls.[1] If
skepticism is true, then the search for God is doomed
from the start. Skepticism rules out faith and makes the
blessed, the eternal life unattainable.[2] Near the end of
Contra Academicos he argues that skepticism leads to an
approval of immorality.[3] It is not surprising, then, that
he writes, "I believe that a thorough search for the truth
is neither a trifling nor a needless occupation for us, but
rather a necessary and important one."[4] Augustine's personal concern with skepticism is even more understandable

because he had experienced in his own life its stultifying effect on the mind.

His major discussion of skepticism is contained in his *Contra Academicos,* which, significantly, was the first work he undertook after his conversion to Christianity.[5] The skepticism Augustine attacks is that advocated by the members of the New Academy, hence the title of the work, "Against the Academicians." The Academic skepticism was primarily opposed to the empiricism of the Stoics, but the Academicians based some of their conclusions on premises they accepted from Zeno the Stoic. They accepted Zeno's definition of truth—that something is understood to be true when it contains no sign of error—but they went beyond Zeno in arguing that nothing can be found that is free from error. They also argued that it is wrong to form opinions about uncertain things. Thus, the truly wise man will refuse to give his assent to anything. For the skeptics a wise man is one who merely seeks truth. He will never be deceived into thinking he has attained truth, for everything is uncertain and unproved, nor will he give his assent to anything, for he could only assent to what is uncertain and thus would fall into error.[6]

Like Cicero,[7] Augustine notes the unpopular implications of this reasoning. If a man refuses to accept anything as certain, he will cease from all activity and the refusal to give assent will paralyze human action, because no man does anything unless he first approves of something.[8] Thus, the skeptic's best example of a wise man would seem to be the man who sleeps all day and completely ignores the duties of life. The skeptics thought that they had an answer to this, however. They claimed that although nothing is certain, some things resemble truth and partake of an element of probability. Thus, they concluded, the man who is wise on Academic grounds

need not be slothful and indifferent to duty, because when he does act, he is simply following the most probable truth.

Augustine finds this notion of probability inconsistent with the Academic's position. He argues that one could not think something probable unless something else were taken as true. Consider, he writes, a man who claims he does not know Romanianus yet still admits that some other man is very much like Romanianus. How could he know this man resembles Romanianus unless he also knows Romanianus? And so, how can the skeptics say they do not know any truth and yet continue to follow probability, which, they say, is like the truth? "The example itself proclaims that the Academics are to be likewise laughed at, for they assert that in life they are following what resembles the true, although they do not know what truth itself is."[9] It will not do then for the Academics to say that they are satisfied with the attainment of probability, since a knowledge of probability is impossible apart from a knowledge of truth.[10]

Augustine makes much of the inconsistency of the skeptic's position. This is seen, for example, when the Academician claims, on the one hand, that he possesses wisdom and argues, on the other, that no man knows anything. Since the belief that knowledge is unattainable seems to imply that wisdom is also impossible, the conjunction of the two points is a contradiction. If a man really is incapable of knowing anything, then he cannot even know whether he is living. How can such a man be called wise? Moreover, how can a man be said to be wise when he does not even know what wisdom is?[11]

The skeptic is guilty of still other inconsistencies. He accepts Zeno's definition that information from the senses can be understood as long as it possesses characteristics that something false would not have. Augustine challenges the skeptic to refute Zeno's definition. If the skeptic

cannot refute it, then there is something the skeptic knows and understands, namely, Zeno's definition. However, if the skeptic should succeed in refuting the definition, which is a basic premise in his argument that nothing can be known, then there is no longer any obstacle to human knowledge. Even if the definition is only probable, it still is either true or false. Even though we may be unable to determine which it is, the disjunction itself (the statement that the definition is either true or false) is true, and skepticism is once again refuted.[12] As Augustine puts this argument in a later writing, "Everyone who knows that he has doubts knows with certainty something that is true, namely, that he doubts. He is certain, therefore, about a truth. Therefore everyone who doubts whether there be such a thing as *the* truth has at least *a* truth to set a limit to his doubt; and nothing can be true except truth be in it."[13]

Augustine observes that though these "observations suffice for gaining victory . . . they are insufficient for a complete rout of the adversary."[14] He recognizes that although his arguments provide a sufficient refutation of the Academic theory, he wants to destroy the position as thoroughly as he can. Accordingly, he seeks to answer the skeptic's charges against sense perception. The Academicians offered many arguments to show the deceptiveness and unreliability of the senses. For example, since it is obvious that the senses deceive us, how can Augustine be so certain that the world exists? Moreover, the relativity of the senses militates against their ability to give us knowledge.[15] To one man a breeze may be pleasant, while to a fevered man the same breeze may be disagreeable. Because sense experience leads to the contradiction that the same wind is both pleasant and unpleasant, how can it be a source of knowledge?

It is interesting to compare Augustine's views on this to those of Plato and Descartes. Plato often pointed to

the deceptiveness of the senses and concluded that they were unable to provide man with knowledge. At best, Plato concluded, the senses could give man opinion. Augustine considers the possibility that the members of the New Academy never departed from Plato's original position, and thus the skeptical Academicians did not really believe the views they taught. The empiricism of the Stoics had to be attacked, and while the Academicians did this, they secretly maintained Plato's views that truth belonged to the intelligible world.[16] When this is coupled with Augustine's views about the truly wise man being not the skeptic, relativist, or empiricist but the Platonist who limits knowledge to the intelligible world,[17] it is surprising that Augustine bothered to come to the defense of sensation. Thus, Augustine's refutation of skepticism did not require a defense of sense experience. He could have ignored or even accepted these arguments and still refuted skepticism by showing the existence of intelligible truths.

There are two possible reasons for Augustine's defense of sense experience against the charges of the skeptics and relativists. The first is theological. He may have realized that one of his religious authorities, the Bible, depended to some extent upon the testimony of many people. If the senses are completely unreliable, then we cannot trust the reports of witnesses who say they heard Jesus teach or saw him die or saw him alive three days after he had been crucified. If it can be proved that no one saw the resurrected Christ, or if it can be shown that the experiences of seeing a risen Christ were necessarily deceptive and unreliable, then the truth of the faith can be seriously challenged.

There may have been another reason for his defense. Even if one grants that the senses sometimes deceive and are unreliable, it does not follow that they always deceive

or are unreliable.[18] Augustine's position on this matter contrasts sharply with that of Descartes. Descartes was so anxious to avoid error that he was willing to settle for a bare minimum of truth; Augustine was more concerned with finding truth, even if this involved accepting some error with it.

Augustine's defense of the senses is illustrated by his remarks in *De civitate Dei*. He writes that the Christian "believes also the evidence of the senses which the mind uses by aid of the body; for if one who trusts his senses is sometimes deceived, he is more wretchedly deceived who fancies he should never trust them."[19]

One of Augustine's moves in answering the skeptic's attack on sensation was to show that there is an element of truth in all sense perception. That is, whenever I perceive that something is red—whether or not it is in fact red—it is true that it appears red to me. Does the oar in water appear bent? If it does and one describes what he sees by saying, "That oar *appears* bent," then what he says is incontrovertible. If we refuse to give assent to anything more than the appearance of something, the truth of what we say cannot be denied, but if we go beyond this and attempt to use the perception as a criterion of truth, it is always fallible. It is only when we go beyond the appearance of the bent oar and affirm that it is really bent, that we are in error.[20]

The senses, then, cannot be blamed for error. Error is the result of the mind's going beyond the data furnished by the senses and assuming that objects really are as they appear.

> Even the eyes do not cause mistakes, for they can report nothing to the mind except what they actually see. If not only the eyes but also all the bodily senses report simply as they are affected, I know not what more we ought to expect of them. . . . Anyone who thinks that

the oar is broken in the water and is restored when it is taken out has nothing wrong with his senses, but he is a bad judge of what they convey to him. . . . Air and water differ, so it is proper that sensations should be different according as they relate to things in air and in water. So the eye does its duty correctly, for it was made simply to see. But the mind operated perversely, for it and not the eye was made to contemplate supreme beauty.[21]

Although the skeptic can sometimes claim that things are other than they appear, he cannot refute Augustine when he describes the way things appear to him. Since Augustine uses the term "world" to refer to whatever is present to his eyes and since there are many things that appear to him in certain ways, Augustine believes the skeptic has no grounds for saying the world does not exist. If the skeptic means what Augustine means by "world," its existence cannot be denied. If he does not mean what Augustine means, then their so-called disagreement about the existence of the world turns out to be nothing more than verbal dispute as to how one should use the term "world."[22]

Augustine next considers the skeptic's appeal to dreams and illusions. As long as dreams and illusions last, they seem as real as the ordinary reports of the senses. Is not the information our senses give us discredited by illusions or dreams? Descartes believed that it is, but Augustine refused to give ground on this issue.

First of all, he is not foolish enough to admit everything we perceive when asleep exists. "Of course, I am not saying that I perceived the same thing that I would perceive if I were awake, but you can say that what I perceive when I am awake could appear to me also when I am asleep."[23] Regardless of how the world seems to us when we are asleep or deranged, Augustine insists that the world[24] as such remains the same, regardless of how it may change

in such delusions.[25] Although none of his remarks so far refute the skeptic's appeal to dreams, he argues that certain truths remain whether we are asleep or awake.

> If there are one world and six worlds, it is clear that there are seven worlds, no matter how I may be affected. And, with all due modesty, I maintain that I know this. . . . I regard it as already sufficiently plain that the things which are seen awry through sleep or derangement are things that pertain to the bodily senses, for even if the whole human race were fast asleep, it would still be necessarily true that *three times three* are nine, and that this is the square of intelligible numbers.[26]

Augustine will not allow, then, that either sleep or the impairment of our senses rules out the possibility of knowing truth. If the senses do an adequate job of intimating to the alert man and the sane man, it is no concern of theirs what the fancies of a sleeping or insane man may be. The fact that deranged persons are deluded or that sleeping people see things incorrectly does not prove that the senses of a vigilant sane man are unreliable.

Augustine finds still another example of certain truth in the principles of logic and mathematics. The skeptic cannot deny that such laws of logic as the law of contradiction[27] or the law of the excluded middle[28] are true. Through dialectic, Augustine writes, "I have learned that these and many other things . . . are true, true in themselves, howsoever our senses may be affected."[29] Nor can the skeptic deny the truths of mathematics for "even if the whole human race were fast asleep, it would still be necessarily true that *three times three* are nine."[30]

But the knowledge we can attain goes beyond abstract logical and mathematical truths. We can also have certain knowledge about real existence, and he offers as his example perhaps the most conclusive of all objections to skepticism. "But, without any illusion of image, fancy, or phantasm, I

am certain that I am, that I know that I am. . . . In the face of these truths, the quibbles of the skeptics lose their force. If they say: "What if you are mistaken?"—well, if *I* am mistaken, I am. For, if one does not exist, he can by no means be mistaken. Therefore, I am, if I am mistaken."[31]

Augustine did not try, as Descartes was to do with his *cogito*, to prove anything on the basis of this argument other than that it is a clear example of an indubitable truth which not even the most serious skeptic can dispute. In order to doubt, I must exist.

So much then for Augustine's refutation of skepticism. Truth does exist and man can attain it.

In Augustine's writings, the word "truth" can describe not only propositions but also the reality to which propositions refer. Augustine draws a crucial distinction between truth *(veritas)* and true things *(verum)*. Just as chastity differs from that which is chaste, so truth is more excellent than things which are true. Augustine notes at least three important differences between *veritas* and *verum*.

(1) True things are particular instances of truth, just as things that are equal are particular instances of equality.[32] This is just another way of stating Plato's point that the particular things of this spatio-temporal world imitate the eternal, intelligible standard.

(2) Truth remains immutable, even though true things change. For example, the ratio that one is to two as two is to four "was no truer yesterday than today, nor will it be truer tomorrow or a year hence. Even if the whole world should fall in ruins, that ratio will always necessarily be: it will always be such as it is now."[33]

(3) Truth is eternal, while true things may perish. Just as equality does not perish when two equal sticks are destroyed, so truth does not cease when true things perish.[34] A good example of this is afforded by nonnecessary proposi-

tions that happen to be true, such as the proposition, "Augustine is now thirty-three years old." When the state of affairs described by the proposition changes (for example, Augustine reaches the age of thirty-four), the original proposition is no longer true. But truth itself is unaffected by the fact that the truth of certain propositions is influenced by conditions of time and change. But, it might be asked, do not contingently true propositions like "I am now eating" undermine Augustine's claim that truth is eternal and immutable? A contemporary reply to this question has been given by Professor George Nakhnikian. He writes, "No doubt it is sometimes true that I am eating and sometimes not true that I am eating. But that is because the sentence 'I am eating' is not sufficient by itself to uniquely indicate a single proposition; hence, these words alone do not indicate anything that is capable of truth or falsity. What is true at one time is that I am eating at that time, and what is not true at another time is that I am eating at that other time, and these are not the same."[35]

Augustine says more about the eternity of truth in Book Two of his *Soliloquies*. He argues that because it is self-contradictory to deny the eternity of truth, truth is logically indestructible. If the world will never pass away, it is true that the world will never pass away. If the world will someday perish, then *that* is true. But truth itself will abide even though every created thing should perish. However, the question might still be asked, "What if truth itself should perish?" Augustine's answer is, "Will it not be true that Truth has perished?"[36] Thus, the very denial of truth's eternity turns out to be an affirmation of its indestructibility.

Our minds do not judge truth; rather truth judges our reason.[37] If truth were inferior to our minds, we would judge it instead of using it as a standard of judgment. We

often judge men's minds when, for example, we say that this mind is not as keen as it might be, but we do not stand in judgment of what is eternal or what is truth. If truth and our minds were equal, it would not be eternal and unchanging, since our minds are finite, mutable, and subject to error. Thus, truth must be more excellent than human reason.[38]

Augustine also argues that truth must exist somewhere; that is, there must be some ontological ground or basis for truth. But surely the ground of truth cannot be anything perishable. Since truth is eternal, it must reside in that which is eternal. "Whatever is, cannot be permanent if that in which it exists is not permanent. A moment ago we agreed that Truth remains even when true things perish. Truth, therefore, does not exist in mortal things. But it must exist somewhere. There are, therefore, immortal things. But nothing is true in which Truth does not exist. Therefore, only immortal things are true."[39] Since God alone is immortal, He must be the ground of truth.

Augustine says that God is more than the ground of truth. Truth partakes of attributes that can belong only to deity, such as eternity and immutability. Thus, Augustine concludes, truth is God. "For where I found truth, there I found my God, who is the Truth itself."[40] It follows then that if man knows truth, he also knows God.

Still one more distinction must be made. It has already been suggested that Augustine finds a difference between truth and true things that partake of truth but that can perish. A distinction must also be made between truth (God) and the eternal truths of mathematics, geometry, ethics, and beauty. These latter truths (which are Augustine's equivalent of the Platonic forms) are the standards used in making judgments in the various disciplines. Though they, like truth, are eternal and immutable, they must in some sense be subordinated to the truth that is

God. Accordingly, Augustine writes, "You will never deny that there is an unchangeable truth which contains everything that is unchangeably true."[41]

The most obvious analogy at this point is Plato's doctrine of the form of the Good. In what may be his most difficult thought to interpret Plato referred to the form of the good as the highest form. He spoke of it as the cause of the other forms.[42] The latter became known only insofar as they were illumined by the idea of good. As Augustine interpreted the form of the good as God,[43] this reminded him of the relationship between his God and the eternal truths. God is the eternal and immutable cause (in the sense of ontological ground) of the forms and the cause (in the sense of efficient cause) of the spatio-temporal world patterned after the forms. The forms or *rationes aeternae* are thus eternal truths and must not be confused with the particular things that are said to be true, but the eternal truths must also be distinguished from the truth that is God.

chapter
three : the role
of faith

Augustine's refutation of skepticism has shown
that truth is attainable by man. The next question is how
man arrives at a knowledge of truth, and Augustine's
answer to this problem begins with his doctrine of faith.
In a certain sense faith is the beginning of knowledge.[1]

"First believe, then understand"[2] is a theme that recurs
throughout Augustine's writings. "We believed that we
might know; for if we wished first to know and then to
believe, we should not be able to know or to believe."[3]
Augustine does not mean by this that we begin with faith
and then go on to knowledge. He is teaching, instead,
that we must believe in order to know. Faith, in a sense,
is a precondition of knowing.[4]

Augustine's teaching on the subject of faith is more
complex than is sometimes recognized. Faith plays notice-
ably different roles insofar as it is related to either *scientia*
or *sapientia*. Furthermore, Augustine uses the word "faith"
in a number of different senses. Unless these various uses
are delineated, Augustine's view of the relationship between faith and reason cannot be fully explored.

Augustine was acquainted with the kind of philosophy
that ridicules any adherence to faith; he had once been
deceived by the Manichees on this very point. In their
claim to follow only reason—apart from authority—the

Manichees had led the young Augustine into thinking that there was something wrong in the exercise of faith. As Augustine describes the trap that ensnared him, "For no other reason we fell in with such men [the Manichees], than because they used to say, that, apart from all terror of authority, by pure and simple reason, they would lead within to God, and set free from all error those who were willing to be the hearers."[5]

Augustine expended much time and effort in refuting this attack on faith. With great care he distinguishes faith from credulity,[6] opinion,[7] and wishful thinking.[8]

Then he turns on the Manichean doctrine. Suppose, he argues, that I decide to follow the Manichean advice to avoid faith. Am I not believing the very man who bids me not to believe? "Therefore, I should not come unto him, who forbids me to believe, unless I believe something. Is there any greater madness, than that I should displease him by faith alone, which is founded on no knowledge, which faith alone led me to him?"[9]

Thus, the Manichean polemic against faith is refuted by the fact that his own argument, if accepted, must be believed. Augustine raises an additional argument, however, in claiming that faith is not peculiar to religion. It is, in fact, indispensable in every area of life. To take a simple example one's knowledge of his own identity depends upon faith, for how else would one know that the people who claim to be his parents really are unless he either trusts their word or the word of someone else?[10] Moreover, all learning depends on faith. If we refused to believe things that we have not experienced personally, we could never know the facts of history, which are based upon the testimony of others whom we take to be authorities. This, Augustine insists, is faith.[11]

If the Manichean is not impressed by these arguments, Augustine shows that a knowledge of other human beings is impossible apart from an exercise of faith. "But, who-

soever thou art who wilt not believe save what thou seest, lo, bodies that are present thou seest with the eyes of the body, wills and thoughts of thine own that are present, because they are in thine own mind, thou seest by the mind itself; tell me, I pray thee, thy friend's will towards thee by what eyes seest thou?"[12]

Thus, although we can see bodies with our physical eyes and see our own thoughts and will by the eyes of our mind, we cannot see the minds of other people. Yet no Manichean seriously maintains that other people have no minds; he sees their physical actions and hears their words, but he takes it for granted that they have minds. This, Augustine informs him, is not sight but faith. "Will you haply say that you see the will of another through his works? Therefore you will see acts and hear words, but, concerning your friend's will, that which cannot be seen and heard you will believe."[13]

Finally, Augustine considers the Manichean criticism of the faith that Christians have in the Bible. He argues, first, that when one abandons the authority of the Scriptures, he does not abandon all authority. The Manichean only substitutes one authority for another, and in this case he sets up his own mind as an authority above the Scriptures. "Instead of making the high authority of Scripture the reason of approval, every man makes his approval the reason for thinking a passage (of Scripture) correct. If, then, you discard authority, to what, poor feeble soul . . . will you betake yourself? Set aside authority, and let us hear the reason of your beliefs."[14]

If the Manichean insists on abandoning all authority, what reasons can he give for his peculiar doctrines, such as that Atlas upholds the earth or that there are eight continents and ten heavens? The only reason offered to support such fictions is the authority of Manichaeus. After the Manichean rejects faith in the Scriptures on the ground that all faith is wrong, he then turns by faith to a

less reliable authority. "If, then, you submit to receive a load of endless fictions at the bidding of an obscure and irrational authority, so that you believe all these things because they are written in books which *your misguided judgment* pronounces trustworthy, though there is no evidence of their truth, why not rather submit to the authority of the Gospel."[15]

Augustine is not saying simply that because the Manichean accepts the dubious teachings of Manichaeus on faith, he should instead accept the teachings of Scripture. His point is more profound. The Manichean set up his own reason as the best judge of truth, but this led him to accept every kind of nonsense. If the Manichean is going to believe something (as he must), he should believe the gospel, the authority of which does not rest on the preferences of individuals. Instead, the authority of the Bible "is so well founded, so confirmed, so generally acknowledged and admired, and . . . has an unbroken series of testimonies from the apostles down to our day, that . . . you may have an intelligent belief."[16] A blind faith (like that of the Manicheans) that is grounded on an unreliable and untested authority is not only worthless but dangerous. It is necessary that we believe something, but we should put our faith in that which is most worthy of belief.

Augustine divides *scientia* into two areas. He writes, "Our knowledge *(scientia)*, therefore, consists of things seen and believed."[17] Knowledge of things seen is reason and of things believed is faith. Gordon Lewis has termed these two divisions of knowledge "immediate *scientia*" and "mediated *scientia*."[18] Immediate *scientia*, or what Augustine calls reason, is what we know directly without relying on the testimony of any authority. Mediated *scientia*, or faith, is not knowledge of things present to our own senses but knowledge accepted on the authority of witnesses who are trustworthy.[19]

Augustine's notion of mediated *scientia* involves the first of several senses in which he uses the word "faith," knowledge acquired from some authority. He gives several reasons why this kind of faith is necessary. For one thing life is so short that if we waited until all our questions were answered, our lives would be over. No man can possibly live long enough to acquire a direct, personal knowledge of all truth.[20] Faith is also necessitated by the natural limitations of human knowledge. None of us is ever in a position to know everything directly; there are always many truths that have to be accepted on the testimony of some authority.

As long as faith is understood in the first sense noted— as acceptance of authority or indirect knowledge—then it is true by definition that faith plays no role in immediate *scientia*. There are two obvious examples of this kind of knowledge. One can know his own soul directly by intuition and one can perceive sense objects directly. It would be a contradiction to assert that faith (in the sense being considered) plays any role in my present perception of a sensible object.

However, there is another sense of the word in which faith does play a part in immediate *scientia*, at least in sense perception. Unless one assumes or presupposes that the senses are reliable, he will not regard the information received through them as knowledge. The Academician's depreciation of sense experience is proof of this. One need not be conscious or aware of the confidence he has in the senses, for example, but when he becomes conscious that he no longer trusts their reports, they will no longer be regarded as a source of knowledge. Thus, if faith is understood as the act of assuming (consciously or unconsciously) that something is the case, there is a sense in which it is indispensable, even for immediate *scientia*. A knowledge of anything depends somewhat upon one's presupposing certain other things. This is, of course, most clear in

geometry, where there can be no knowledge until certain axioms and postulates are assumed. This is just as true of other areas of knowledge. For example, the Thomist thinks he can reason his way to God's existence without faith. Perhaps he can, in a particular way, but he would not succeed if he had no confidence (faith, in another sense of the word) in the reports of his senses or in the laws of logic.

Thus, although faith in the sense of indirect knowledge plays no role in immediate *scientia*—it would be a contradiction to assert it did—another use of faith becomes apparent, and even in the area of immediate knowledge, one must believe before he can understand.

In relating faith and mediated *scientia*, Augustine uses "faith" in a third way. "For what is believing but consenting to the truth of what is said?"[21] Or, as he put it in one of his last works, "Even belief itself is nothing else than to think with assent."[22] When one accepts something as true on the testimony of some authority, he is giving his assent to what that authority has said. This applies to all areas of mediated knowledge. When the young mathematics student first accepts his teacher's word that forty times ten is four hundred, he is consenting to the truth of what his teacher says. When the history student accepts it as fact that Brutus murdered Caesar, he gives his assent to certain statements he reads in a history book. When a Christian expresses his belief that God was incarnate in Christ, he is likewise accepting as true certain statements of an authority, in this case the Scriptures or the creeds of the church.

With the three senses of faith[23] and their relation to *scientia* Augustine's understanding of the relationship between faith and reason can now be described. There are at least three ways in which reason may be said to precede faith.

First, only creatures capable of reasoning are able to

believe.²⁴ The ability to reason is a necessary condition for believing.²⁵ Second, reason comes before faith in the sense that before one can believe, one must know or understand what it is he is to believe. No one can believe what he does not understand.²⁶ Finally, reason comes before faith because before one believes he is often required to evaluate authority. "We have got to consider whom we have to believe, and the highest (authority) belongs to truth when it is clearly known."²⁷ Augustine in one place describes faith as a resting of the soul in truths that are worthy of belief.²⁸ This implies that our authority must be tested by reason to see whether or not it is reliable. The same passage suggests that the value of faith varies in proportion to the credibility of the authority.

Therefore, Augustine uses both "faith" and "reason" in different senses. Faith serves various functions insofar as it is related to either immediate or mediated *scientia*. As the various aspects of Augustine's teaching become apparent, it is possible to understand how he could assert both that faith precedes reason and that reason precedes faith.

Comparatively little needs to be said in relation to faith and immediate *sapientia*. One reason is that the most important instance of immediate *sapientia* is the knowledge of God that the soul will attain in the beatific vision.²⁹ For the souls that attain this state of blessedness in the life to come the need for faith will cease. In this life believers walk by faith, not by sight, but for those who attain the vision of God faith will be turned into sight.

Although it is true that the need for faith will vanish in the glory of the soul's contemplation of God, the notion of faith is not entirely irrelevant to immediate *sapientia*. For one thing faith plays a necessary role in the progress of the soul toward *contemplatio*. Furthermore, Augustine holds out the possibility of immediate

sapientia in this life, not only through mystical experiences but also through the vision of the divine ideas. *Sapientia* includes man's apprehension of eternal, unchangeable reality, and therefore a knowledge of the forms qualifies as wisdom. Thus, faith is relevant to immediate wisdom.

Finally Augustine relates faith to mediated *sapientia*. Some of the ways in which *sapientia* is mediated are the incarnation and the teachings of Christ, the Bible, and the church. There are several ways that faith aids man in the attainment of *sapientia*.

The usage of "faith" as assent has been noted in connection with the soul's assent to the statements of credible witnesses. If Augustine believes something Romanianus tells him, he is assenting to the truth of Romanianus' statement. Likewise, when one believes the Scriptures or the teachings of the church, he is assenting to the truth of its statements. This last point is important because of the tendency among contemporary theologians to deny any propositional content to revelation.[30] Alan Richardson, for example, speaks disparagingly of those who equate religious faith with belief in certain propositions. Though this warning may be necessary, he continues, "Faith for St. Augustine is not intellectual assent to certain scriptural propositions; it is the awakening of the mind to truth, a new way of seeing things, a means of understanding what before did not make sense, the acquiring of categories of interpretation by means of which our whole experience and thought become rational and coherent."[31] Richardson's opinion ignores much that Augustine wrote concerning faith. Augustine undoubtedly thought of faith as an inward awakening of the mind to truth, but he also taught that the awakening must be grounded on a faith (in the sense of assent) in the statements of the Scriptures and the church. The kind of inward faith that Richardson talks about cannot exist in a vacuum; one necessary condition of faith (in Richard-

son's sense) is a knowledge of certain things about God which are found in the teachings of the Scriptures and the church.

In writing to Jerome, Augustine said:

> I confess to our Charity that I have learned to yield this respect and honour only to the canonical books of Scripture: of these alone do I most firmly believe that the authors were completely free from error. . . . Better far that I should read with certainty and persuasion of its truth the Holy Scripture, placed on the highest (even heavenly) pinnacle of authority, and should, (accept) without questioning the trustworthiness of its statements.[32]

Further support for the claim that Augustine sometimes understood faith as assent to the teachings of Scripture is found in *De libero arbitrio*. There he argues that a man ought to "believe that God exists because that is taught in the books of great men who have left their testimony in writing that they lived with the Son of God, and because they have written that they saw things which could not have happened if there were no God."[33] Augustine's reasoning is not offered as a paradigm of good argumentation, but the statement does support the claim being made. Faith is mediated to man when man has faith in the statements of Scripture. Of course, faith is more than assent to the truths contained in the Bible, but certainly it is not less.

Some things can and must be understood before they can be believed. In *De diversis quaestionibus* Augustine qualifies this by pointing out that some doctrines of the Christian faith must be believed before they can be understood adequately.[34] In still another work he writes:

> For some kinds of things are those which we do not believe, save we understand them; and other kinds of things are those which we do not understand, save we

believe them. For since "faith cometh by hearing, and hearing by the word of Christ" (Rom. 10:17), how can one believe him who preaches the faith, if he—to say nothing of other points—understands not the very tongue which he speaks? But unless, on the other hand, there were some things which we cannot understand, unless we believe them first, the prophet would not say, "If you will not believe, you shall not understand."[35]

Augustine points out that reason is unable to grasp the meaning of a few important Christian doctrines. In these cases we should "let faith precede reason, by which faith the heart may be purified so as to receive and bear the light of the great reason . . . (for) it is reasonable that, with reference to certain great things which cannot yet be grasped, faith should precede reason."[36]

Thus, faith precedes reason in cases where the object of faith is such that reason may occasionally be able to grasp it, but cannot do so at once. In cases where reason is able to understand at once, faith follows reason.

Augustine takes care to distinguish between faith that is a mere mental assent to statements and faith that is a more complete assent of the entire man. This latter type is illustrated in *Contra Academicos* when Augustine tells Romanianus that he will not see truth unless he "devotes himself entirely" to a study of philosophy.[37] In a later work he writes, "For if wisdom and truth are not sought for with the whole strength of the mind, it cannot possibly be found."[38]

Robert E. Cushman, in discussing this aspect of Augustine's thought, distinguishes between *cognitio* (an objective awareness of something) and *agnitio* (acknowledgment)[39] He explains that acknowledgment or re-cognition is always subject to the will. Man's cognitive faculty is relatively neutral or passive with regard to what it receives, but faith, directing the will, leads reason to acknowledge or re-cognize what it recognizes. Since man's will is cor-

rupt and needs cleansing, this kind of knowing is limited to the extent that man receives God's grace. "The passage, therefore, from knowledge to acknowledgment, from philosophy to Christianity, is the transition . . . from 'presumption' to 'confession'. . . . it is a movement away from the standpoint of autonomous reason, as yet unhumbled by the Mediator, to a willing recognition of God in which reason is operative but at length, being cleansed, unambivalently and vigorously lays holds of God, not as an object but in eager and living conversation."[40]

Faith has a role in cleansing the soul. Aristotle subordinated the practical reason to the theoretical reason. For Aristotle man can have purely objective knowledge because, in his words, "Mind as speculative never thinks what is practicable, it never says anything about an object to be avoided or pursued."[41] Augustine opposed this view and argued that the practical reason directs and guides the theoretical reason. The will exercises a great influence on the understanding.[42] Knowing requires that we first want to know. "The bringing forth of the mind is preceded by some desire, by which, through seeking and finding what we wish to know, the off-spring, viz., knowledge itself is born."[43] In other words, the soul must be motivated by some desire in its quest for wisdom and knowledge.[44] Augustine's term for this desire is will (voluntas).

The will's influence upon the understanding can be seen in the case of man's knowledge of God. The rationalistic approach to God attempts to have Him in the mind without also having Him in the heart. This approach will always fail, however, because it does not really desire to find God. Man cannot remain uncommitted until he finds God. God will forever remain undiscovered until man first becomes committed. Augustine's teaching here is similar to that advanced by Jesus in the Gospel according to John: "If any man willeth to do his [God's] will, he shall know of the doctrine."[45] The point of this

text is that an adequate knowledge of Jesus' authority depends upon a willingness to obey his teaching. Truth, then, becomes accessible only when the complete person— the thinking, feeling, and willing individual—turns to the truth that is God.

Thus, even though man's intellectual capacities are capable of attaining mediated *sapientia*, their possession is not a sufficient condition for its attainment. These rational capacities are helpless unless they are used, and the will is the part of man's soul that moves him to use his mind. Hence, the motions of the will—love and desire—play a necessary role in the attainment of *sapientia*.[46] "To enjoy the Wisdom of God, however, implies nothing else than to cleave to the same in love. Neither does any one abide in that which he apprehends, but by love."[47]

The introduction of the notion of love raises another point. The will influences the intellect, but the will in turn is moved by love. Just as bodies tend to fall because of their weight, souls tend toward that which they love.[48] In his *Confessions* Augustine expresses this in his famous words, "My weight is my love; by it am I borne whithersoever I am borne."[49] Man's will is, then, influenced by man's love. However, there is within man a principle or force that incessantly pulls him down, to make him love the lesser good. Sin hinders man's ability to attain *sapientia* because it "causes a swelling under which corruption gathers, and spreads out over the eye of the mind to prevent it from seeing the richness of truth."[50]

In *De libero arbitrio* Augustine notes that two penal conditions afflict the sinful soul—ignorance and difficulty. "From ignorance springs disgraceful error, and from difficulty comes painful effort. To approve falsehood instead of truth so as to err in spite of himself, and not be able to refrain from the works of lust because of the pain involved in breaking away from fleshly bonds: these do not belong to the nature of man as he was created. *They*

are the penalty of man as condemned."⁵¹ Ignorance is
natural to man; it is a result of the fall of man. If man,
through the stubborn sinfulness of his own will, refuses
to take means to progress toward knowledge, however, he
falls into an even worse state of ignorance, which is penal.
A man cannot be held guilty for his natural ignorance.
But he is guilty when as a result of his persistent refusal
to learn, he fails to attain knowledge.⁵² Thus, the per-
version of man's will even explains man's frequent failure
to gain *scientia.*

The soul is in need of purification. "Now whosoever
supposes that he can know truth while he is still living
iniquitously, is in error."⁵³ This position does not lead
to a *de jure* skepticism. It would if man could not under
any circumstances progress toward knowledge or wisdom,
but knowledge becomes attainable because God's grace can
overcome man's natural sluggishness in knowing. Divine
grace is the cure for the noetic effects of sin. Augustine
praises God because He gave man "the power to rise from
such beginnings to ability to attain the chief good. He
renders aid as he [man] advances. He [God] completes
and perfects his [man's] advance."⁵⁴ But it is important
to notice also that sin affects chiefly man's capacity for
sapientia, not for *scientia.* One does not have to be a
Christian to know the law of gravity, but he does need
faith if he is to relate the principles of nature to their
eternal creator. When Augustine says that a man cannot
know truth while living iniquitously, he must not be
understood as referring to true things. He must mean
that unless we are cleansed from sin, we cannot know
the truth that is God. Although a man's moral condition
may be irrelevant to his attainment of *scientia, sapientia*
is unattainable apart from a righteous life.

> But when the soul has properly adjusted and disposed
> itself, and has rendered itself harmonious and beautiful,

then will it venture to see God, the very source of all truth and the very Father of Truth. . . . Since we are to enjoy to the full that Truth which lives without change and since, in that Truth, God the Trinity, the Author and Founder of the universe, takes counsel for the things which He has created, the mind must be cleansed in order that it may be able to look upon that light and cling to it when it has seen it.[55]

One qualification that must be made is that Augustine did allow men a measure of *sapientia* without faith. For example, Augustine admits that "the Platonists" attained an understanding of the eternal truths. This is undoubtedly a result of an aspect of God's grace that later theologians termed "common grace." However, whatever wisdom man can attain apart from faith is limited, and inadequate to bring man to a knowledge of the source of truth, God Himself. Even this limited *sapientia* is possible only because "the Platonists," and others like them who may attain it, manage to free themselves from the hindrances of the body and sensation.

The analysis of Augustine's several uses of "faith" has the advantage of isolating these uses along with the different functions they perform with regard to *scientia* and *sapientia*, but it also raises a problem. Unless there is a univocal element common to these various uses, Augustine's entire discussion of faith seems tainted by equivocation. If the several meanings of "faith" have nothing in common, why use the same word to describe them?

Perhaps the term "faith" does have a univocal meaning that is common to Augustine's uses of it. If faith is defined to mean an assent of the soul to truths thought[56] worthy of belief, much of this problem will vanish. Thus, in the case of the first sense of faith noted,[57] faith would be assent to the testimony of witnesses. Reason, of course, must examine the reliability of the authority or witness.

This faith comes before knowledge in the sense that we can know very little directly and thus we must believe (rely on the testimony of others) in order to understand. This faith consists first of assent to the proposition "This authority is reliable," and then of assent to the declarations of that authority.

In regard to faith and the acceptance of certain assumptions or presuppositions the same thing applies. The soul gives its assent to certain statements that serve as assumptions or postulates that influence or govern other things that they think they know. An example of this is the individual who accepts uncritically a naturalistic (as opposed to a supernaturalistic) view of reality.[58] Such an individual will interpret everything in terms of nontheistic categories. Thus, the same evidence that seems, to a theist, to establish the existence of God or the occurrence of a certain miracle will fail to convince the naturalist unless he should abandon his naturalistic assumptions. Sometimes (as in the assumption of the laws of logic) the soul gives its assent to these postulates, even though they cannot be proved. At other times, such as in the belief that the senses are reliable, the soul may continue to give its assent because it has never thought to question the belief.

chapter
four : sensation

Augustine distinguishes three levels of perception or vision—corporeal, spiritual, and intellectual vision. This chapter will concentrate on Augustine's teachings about corporeal vision or sense perception. However, Augustine did not think that corporeal vision and spiritual vision could be separated in man.[1] It is not simply man's body that senses; rather, man's soul senses through his body.

It is always important to see Augustine's teaching in terms of the influence that earlier philosophers may have had on him, and this is especially important in connection with his theory of sensation. Many of Augustine's views seem odd and even patently false to the mind unacquainted with his philosophic milieu. As Augustine's doctrines are compared and contrasted with, for example, those advanced by Plotinus against the Aristotelian, Stoic, and Epicurean epistemologies, Augustine's views become if not plausible at least more intelligible.

Both Augustine and Plotinus were driven to several of their conclusions about sensation by their views about man's soul and body. Plotinus rejected both the materialistic theories of the soul advanced by the Stoics and Epicureans and Aristotle's view that the soul is the form of the body.[2] For Plotinus the soul is a substance that exists in its own right; that is, it can exist independently of

the body. Sensation depends upon the immortal and immaterial soul working in harmony with the body. "The soul, in the feeling, may be compared to the workman in such operations as boring or weaving, the body to the tool employed: the body is passive and menial; the soul is active."[3]

In a similar vein Augustine defines man as a "rational substance consisting of mind and body."[4] The soul is that which gives life to the body;[5] it is a substance, sharing in reason, which is suited to rule the body.[6] As Vernon Bourke describes it, Augustine's view of body and soul is "a one-way or unilateral interactionism,"[7] the soul able to affect the body but the body never able to affect the soul. Augustine regards sensation as a case of the soul making use of its body.[8] Sensation is always a property of the soul, never the body. The body does not feel. Rather, the soul feels through the body.[9]

Thus, for both Plotinus and Augustine, the soul is superior to the body and as such cannot be affected by the physical organism. If there is any influence between body and soul, it must come from the higher (the soul) to the lower (the body).

Augustine agreed with Plato and Plotinus that the senses alone cannot supply knowledge. He writes that the Platonists[10] "are beyond all comparison with those who taught that the criterion of truth is in the bodily senses, and who would have us believe that all knowledge is to be measured and ruled by such doubtful and deceitful testimony."[11] Augustine's criticism is especially directed at the Epicureans and Stoics, who thought that the notions needed for the unification of knowledge were derivable from sensation. In contrast Augustine insists that the canons of truth, beauty, and goodness cannot be derived from sensation alone. However, he makes it clear that neither he nor the Platonists are rejecting sensation; they are only putting it in its proper place. "Certainly,

the Platonists whom we rightly prefer to all others, were able to distinguish what is apprehended by the mind from what is apprehended by the senses, without either denying or exaggerating the faculties of sense."[12]

Sense perception is not knowledge. "For, to perceive by the senses is one thing, but to *know* is something else. Wherefore, if we know anything, I think it is contained in the intellect alone, and by it alone can it be grasped."[13] We cannot and should not expect truth from sensation, for the primary function of sensation is not to picture for the mind what things are like but to warn the soul of changes in the body. Since sensible things are mutable,[14] how can one expect them to provide immutable truth? Augustine remained convinced that knowledge must have the unchangeable as its object. "Do you not know," he wrote, "that some philosophers, and very good thinkers, too, thought that not even what is grasped by the mind is worthy of the name of knowledge, unless that comprehension is so firm that the mind cannot be moved from it by any argument?"[15]

A most important discussion of the difference between sensation and knowledge occurs in *De quantitate animae*. Augustine notes that while animals can sense,[16] they do not have a reason and thus cannot possess knowledge.[17] Evodius at first finds himself unwilling to accept this conclusion. After all, we sometimes speak of animals as if they have knowledge, as for example, when we say that a dog *knows* his master.[18] Augustine accepts the challenge that this poses to his view that knowledge is not sense perception. He proceeds first to lead Evodius to see that "knowledge implies the perception of something with certainty."[19] He then shows Evodius the absurd consequences that result from allowing brutes the possession of knowledge. Granting that brutes have the power to know implies that they have a higher form of life than man, because they could possess knowledge without also

possessing a reason.[20] Evodius is satisfied that animals cannot know, but he still requests an explanation of the case in which a dog is said to know his master. Augustine answers, "Many animals surpass us in sense perception . . . but in mind and reason and knowledge God has placed us over them. The sense perception of animals, aided by the great force of habit enables them to pick out the things that satisfy their souls, and this is done all the more easily because the brute soul is more closely bound to the body."[21] Thus, the dog's awareness of his master is accounted for by the dog's greater capacity of sense perception that is accompanied by habit or reinforced experience. Sensation in brutes is always directed toward some activity—usually the seeking of pleasure or the avoiding of pain.[22] Man, however, has the ability to judge his sensations on the basis of eternal ideas and to direct his awareness of sensation to *scientia*.

The fact that man can produce *scientia* from sensation accounts for numerous passages where Augustine asserts the importance of sensation. In *De Trinitate* he admits that "not only our own senses, but those of other persons also have added very much indeed to our knowledge." In the same passage he continues, "Far be it from us to doubt the truth of what we have learned by the bodily senses; since by them we have learned to know the heaven and the earth, and those things in them which are known to us."[23] How else could we know that the ocean, cities, and lands exist unless we trusted either our own senses or those of others? Knowledge of sensible objects is the kind of thing that practical living finds indispensable. But while the practical man must not ignore the realm of the sensible, he must at the same time be warned that too much concentration on the sensible to the exclusion of a study of the intelligible will keep him from the proper object of true knowledge, that which is eternal and immutable.

Aristotle, the Epicureans, and the Stoics had all understood sensation in a passive sense. They thought the soul received impressions from the senses. Plotinus rejected all three forms of a passive theory of sensation.[24] Included among his objections was his argument that if the objects of perception are in the soul (which would be the case if the soul's knowledge of sensible objects is limited to impressions imprinted upon it), then the soul will be unable to make judgments of distance.[25] In order for the soul to see there must be a distance between the eye and the object. That this is the case can be shown by pressing some object one desires to see against the eyeball. When there is no distance between the organ of sight and the object, sight cannot occur. Thus, Plotinus concludes, the soul cannot *see* any impression that has been stamped upon it. He argued further that an impressionistic theory of sensation cannot account for memory.[26] In the passive view memory would have to be a preservation of some sense impression. But if the impression ever completely ceased, it could not be remembered, and if it never ceased, it would never be forgotten. Obviously, though, we can bring into our memory things that were forgotten. Finally Plotinus presents what he believes to be the most convincing objection to a passive theory of sensation. "If to see is to accept imprints of the objects of our vision, we can never see these objects themselves; we see only vestiges they leave within us, shadows: the things themselves would be very different from our vision of them."[27]

Augustine also rejects the view that in sensation the soul passively receives images from the outer world through the instrumentality of the senses. He follows Plotinus in understanding the soul's role in sensation as active. Both the images associated with particular sensations and the intellectual ideas corresponding to them are brought into being by the activity of the soul. Sensation belongs not

to the body but to the soul. "When we see a body and its image begins to exist in our soul, it is not the body that impresses the image in our soul. It is the soul itself that produces it with wonderful swiftness within itself."[28]

Augustine's teaching concerning the relation between the soul and sensation is one of the more difficult elements of his thought. He regards the senses as the corporeal instruments through which the soul perceives.[29] The power of sensation is exercised when the soul intensifies its activity in a particular sense organ.[30] Sensation occurs when the soul notices and concentrates its activity and attention upon a passion, disturbance, or corporeal motion in the body.[31]

From another viewpoint, external bodies act upon the sense organs of the body. Since the soul is always attentive to modifications in the body, it is immediately aware of them and makes from its own spiritual substance an image corresponding to the modification in the body. Augustine calls this image a sensation.

> In short, it seems to me the soul, when it has sensations in the body, is not affected in any way by it, but it pays more attention to the passions of the body. But this sense, even while we do not sense, being nevertheless in the body, is an instrument of the body directed by the soul for its ordering so the body may be more prepared to act on the passions of the body with attention to the end of joining like things to like and of repelling what is harmful.[32]

Thus, the various kinds of sensation occur when the soul attends to changes in the body. Augustine apparently believes that sensible objects affect the bodily sense either directly, as in touch, or through some medium, as in hearing.

Augustine, therefore, concurs with Plotinus that the soul plays an active role in sensation, but he strangely does not take advantage of Plotinus' objections to the

passive theory. The only explicit objection Augustine makes is given in Book Six of *De musica*. The master tells his disciple to be amazed at the idea of the body's being able to affect or influence the soul. Instead, "the soul does not receive from the body, but receiving from God on high it rather impresses on the body."[33] Later in the same book the master asks whether hearing depends upon something being produced in the soul by the body. Augustine objects to this because such a view would subordinate a superior substance, the soul, to an inferior substance, the body. He finds it difficult to conceive of a more detestable belief.[34] But, the disciple asks, if hearing is not the result of the body's producing something in the soul, what is it? The master replies simply that whatever our answer is, we must not subordinate the soul to the body.

Augustine's argument as it stands seems inadequate, because he never seems to examine the assumption that influence can proceed only from a higher to a lower level. Although this may be true as far as God is concerned, it does not follow so clearly in the case of man's soul. Apparently even Augustine was not happy with his argument, because he writes, "If, because of the infirmity of either or both of us, the result [of our investigation into the nature of sensation] should be less than we wish, either we ourselves shall investigate it at another time when we are less agitated, or we shall leave it to more intelligent people to examine, or, unworried, *we shall leave it unsolved.*"[35]

Whether or not Plotinus' arguments were more conclusive, he at least presented a more substantial case against the passive theory of sensation. It is interesting to theorize why Augustine did not make greater use of Plotinus' arguments. There is no reason to believe that Augustine objected to Plotinus' reasoning. After all, they were confronting a common enemy, and Plotinus' argu-

ments do not, as was the case with his viewpoints on many other issues, hold implications inconsistent with Augustine's Christianity. The only other likely answer is that Augustine was unacquainted with those sections of the *Enneads* that contained Plotinus' refutation of the passive theory.

However, though Augustine presents only one explicit argument against the passive theory, clearly one more reason underlies his thought. Augustine associated a passive theory of sensation with materialism. While he had never been a Stoic or an Epicurean, he had been involved personally in the errors of another type of materialism, Manicheanism. Since he rejected Manichean materialism and emphasized the spiritual nature of the soul, it would have been unlikely that he would advance a passive theory. Even this point does not substantially strengthen his case, however. Had he been more familiar with Aristotle's epistemology, he might have realized that a passive theory of sensation and a materialistic metaphysics need not go together.

The Epicureans, Stoics, and to some degree even Aristotle had held mechanistic views of sensation, though there were differences among them. The Epicureans followed Democritus and argued for a changing medium, a stream of atoms passing from the object to the sense organ. Aristotle and Stoics argued for a more continuous medium.

Plotinus rejected all the mechanistic accounts of sensation and their postulations of a medium between the object and the sense organ.[36] He argued that if there were such a medium, it would only dull one's sensations. Sensation, he claimed, is an example of action at a distance. Furthermore, if an object of perception, for example, a tree, affected not our sense organ but first the air, then what we see would be not the tree but the air. Plotinus' rejection of a materialistic medium between a

sense organ and its sensible object confronted him with the problem of finding an alternative explanation of how a sensible quality can affect a sense organ though separated by distance from that organ. His answer was his famous theory of sympathy.

> The whole matter seems to bring us back to that sympathy of which we have treated. If a certain thing is of a nature to be sympathetically affected by another in virtue of some similitude between them; then anything intervening, not sharing in that similitude, will not be affected, or at least not similarly. If this be so, anything naturally disposed to be affected will take the impression more vividly in the absence of intervening substance, even of some substance capable itself of being affected.[37]

Plotinus' theory is largely unintelligible without the knowledge that he understood the world organically and not mechanistically. "Perception of every kind seems to depend on the fact that our universe is a whole sympathetic to itself: that it is so, appears from the universal participation in power from member to member, and especially in remote power."[38] In Plotinus' universe separation is effected by difference and not by distance.[39] The sense organ and the sensible object are linked by universal sympathy.

Augustine gives the impression of being undecided on the entire issue. His understanding of sensation—the soul's awareness of modifications in the body—has already been noted. But how does he explain the way in which external objects separated from the body by space manage to affect the body?

Augustine takes up the subject for the first time in *De quantitate animae*.[40] He points out to Evodius that while Augustine's body is in one place and Evodius' body is in another, Evodius' eyes still perceive Augustine's body. "But your eyes perceive my body and, if they perceive, they certainly experience. Again they cannot there ex-

perience, where what they experience is not. Yet, your eyes are not there where my body is. Therefore, they experience where they are not."[41] To solve this difficulty Augustine in this work appeals to the ray theory of sight. According to this view, the eye emits a ray of light that brings the sense organ into immediate contact with the object. If it is not our eyes that perceive, perhaps it is sight. "And so it is, for sight goes forth and through the eyes shines far to light up what we see. Hence it follows that there it sees where the object is which it sees, and not at the point where it goes out to see. It is not you, then, that see, when you see me."[42]

In another work written during this same general time in his life[43] he suggests that a medium, such as a medium of vibrating air is necessary to affect the ear and make hearing possible.[44] This raises the immediate problem of understanding how the ray theory, which brings the body into immediate contact with the sensible object, can be reconciled with theory of a medium. There are several possible answers. It might be claimed that since sensation is the soul's immediate awareness of bodily modifications, neither the ray nor the medium are necessary for sensation. This move apparently attempts to avoid the difficulty by making the question of perception at a distance irrelevant to sensation. But it clearly will not do, for it can be asked, could there be sensation (for Augustine) without a physical change in the sense organ? Augustine's answer is no.[45] Could the bodily modification take place without a sensible object affecting it in some way? Once again, Augustine answers negatively. If the bodily modification depends upon some action of the sensible object, then sensation is also dependent. If either a medium or a ray is necessary to produce the bodily effect (even though this effect is not itself the sensation), then the medium or ray is necessary for sensation.

Another possible solution for the apparent inconsistency

between the ray theory and the medium is that Augustine advances the notion of a ray to explain sight at a distance and the concept of a medium to explain hearing. While this avenue of escape may be open to Augustine, a careful reading of the texts does not suggest that he deliberately drew this fine a distinction.

It is possible that Augustine did not know how to explain perception at a distance and thus wavered between contradictory answers. The subject is reconsidered in *Epistle* 137, and Augustine's remarks in this letter strongly suggest that this answer may be the most accurate.

In *Epistle* 137 Augustine asks how do we perceive things outside our bodies when our soul remains within the body? We can see the stars or sun in heaven, even though there is a great distance between them and our sense organs. The same problem arises with regard to hearing. "Take the case of hearing. This sense spreads outside the body in some way. Why do we say: 'It sounds out-doors,' if we do not hear where the sound is? Do we, then, on that account, live outside our flesh, or can we also experience sensation where we do not live, although sensation cannot exit without life?"[46]

The senses of taste and touch do not bother him particularly,[47] but he continues to return to the singular question raised by seeing and hearing. How can the soul perceive beyond its range of life, or how can it live where it does not exist? Even though the soul can perceive beyond the body, it seems to exist only within the body. Augustine in *Epistle* 137 considers three possible answers for the problem of sight at a distance. First, he asks, "Is seeing not a faculty of perception, although sight is preeminent among the five senses?"[48] It is not clear what he means. Even though sight is the most important of the five senses, he considers the denial that seeing is a faculty of perception.

As a second possibility, he asks, has the soul "sense-

perception beyond the range of its life, and, although it lives only in its own flesh, it also sees things contained in those places outside its own flesh, things which it touches by sight?"[49] This seems to be an allusion to the ray theory of sight. The soul can sense beyond the present confines of the body because the body by means of the ray touches the things that it sees.

Finally, he writes, perhaps the soul "lives in heaven, also, because it perceives what is in heaven, and there can be no sense-perception where there is no life."[50] This statement is interesting because it suggests as an answer to how the soul can perceive where it is not that the soul is present at the point of perception. Thus, perhaps the soul is not confined to the body. This statement could be regarded as a hint that Augustine considered the view of a world soul as a possible solution to the problem of sight at a distance. While Augustine never refers to the Plotinian doctrine of sympathy, he does on occasion speak of a "world soul." For example, he writes, "Reason is a mental operation capable of distinguishing and connecting the things that are learned. But, only a rare class of men is capable of using it as a guide to the knowledge of God or of the soul; either of the soul within us or the world-soul."[51]

Again in *De immortalitate animae* he explains that "the body subsists through the soul and exists by the very fact that it is animated, whether universally, as is the world, or individually, as is each and everything that has life within the world."[52] Augustine neither approves of nor rejects this position in his *Retractions*; instead, he admits that his opinion about a world soul was rash, "not because I can affirm this to be false, but because I do not understand it to be true that the world is something living."[53]

Although Augustine did not mention the possibility of a universal sympathy between the parts of creation, such a notion is but one step removed from a belief in

a world soul. It might possibly be argued that the views of a world soul and a universal sympathy imply a pantheism that is radically inconsistent with Augustine's belief in a transcendent God, but this claim cannot be supported. For one thing Plotinus' God—The One—was transcendent, and yet Plotinus believed in the existence of a world soul and a universal sympathy. Whatever Augustine means by world soul, it is not God but a creature.[54] There would have been no inconsistency in Augustine's asserting both the transcendence of God and the existence of a world soul, created by God, which plays a part in the governing or sustaining of the world. Nor would a doctrine of universal sympathy have been inconsistent with Augustine's view of creation. His teaching about the seminal reasons suggests that his view of physics was not mechanistic. In addition to the ray and medium theories then there are hints that Augustine considered an answer similar to the one proposed by Plotinus—that there is a world soul which ties together the various aspects of creation.

The real source of Augustine's difficulty is his active theory of sensation, the view that in sensation the soul acts instead of being acted upon. If sensation is regarded as an awareness on the part of the soul of a physical change in the sense organ and if the sense organ "sees" an object separated from it by some distance, then the soul must perceive at the point where the sense organ sees. "Certainly, it perceives where it sees, because to see is to perceive; and it perceives where it hears, because to hear is to perceive. Therefore, its life either extends that far, and by this fact it exists there, too, or its perception extends beyond its range of life, or its life is found even where it does not also exist."[55]

Augustine's conclusion to this discussion is disappointing to those who desire a clear solution. He left the problem of perception at a distance with the statement, "All these are a strange amount of absurdity."[56]

While Plotinus refused to allow for any medium between the sense organ and the object, he believed that the sense organ itself serves as a medium between the object and the soul. Plotinus admitted that in sensation alterations or modifications of something take place, but they cannot take place in the soul.[57] While, for example, in the act of seeing, the soul is active, the physical sense organ (in this case, the eye) is passive. Insofar as sensation is related to the sense organ, then, sensation is physical motion, a chemical change in the retina. But this, Plotinus contends, is sensation only in a lower or derivative sense.[58] Plotinus defines sensation in its primary sense as follows: "The perception of sensible objects is the grasping of qualities attaching to bodies by the soul, or by the living being, when it is conscious of them and makes a copy of them on itself."[59] Thus, sensation is a result of the soul, which he compares to an artisan, cooperating with the body, its instrument.[60] The soul does this by giving to each organ the power necessary to do the work for which it is best suited.[61] In the case of the ears the soul gives them the power to hear. Thus, the soul uses the body to grasp corporeal objects.[62]

However, Plotinus did not regard the sense organ as a sufficient condition for sensation to occur. "An organ is not sufficient for vision or for sensation of any kind. The soul must be inclined toward the sensible objects. . . . And when we are engrossed in intellectual objects, sight and the other sensations escape our attention; and in general if we attend to one thing, we miss the others."[63] Although the sense organ is not sufficient for sensation, it is necessary. Without sense organs the soul could not distinguish among the many kinds of sensation; it could not perceive the difference between odors, sights, and sounds. Without sense organs the soul could grasp only its own content, and this would be intellection, not sensation. If other things are to be perceived, the soul must

in some way possess them, but this can be done only as the soul becomes similar to its objects or is related to something else similar. The soul cannot become similar, because it is incorporeal and its objects are corporeal. But the sense organ by sympathy can be modified just as its objects are.[64]

It is difficult to see how this analysis solved Plotinus' problem, however. His efforts seem to move the question back one step. If we grant that an immaterial soul cannot perceive changes in external sensible objects, how can it perceive changes in a physical sense organ? "The disparity between soul and object is halved by the organ; the disparity between organ and object is halved by the visual ray; the disparity between organ and soul is halved by this nature and so one is to leap across the Grand Canyon by jumping half the distance first."[65] As Gordon Clark points out, Plotinus was forced by logical necessity to a position roughly similar to that taken by Philo and others, the postulation of mediators between soul and matter.

Augustine also regards the sense organ as a necessary condition for the perception of corporeal objects. In his seventh epistle he considers a view raised by Nebridius that the soul can have images of corporeal objects, even though it is deprived of the bodily senses.[66] Augustine answers,

> If the soul, before it has the use of the senses for perceiving corporeal things, can imagine those things, and can form better images of them before it becomes entangled in the deceitful senses—which no sane person contends—then the minds of sleepers have more correct images than the minds of persons awake, and insane people are better off than those in mental health; for they would have the images antecedent to those produced by the unreliable senses; and either the sun they see in their minds will be more like the original than the one seen by persons who are sane and awake, or false things are preferable to true ones.[67]

The absurdity of these consequents proves the falsity of the view that sense organs are not necessary. But while sense organs are necessary for corporeal vision, they are not sufficient. Other conditions that must be met include the presence of a sensible object, an act of the will that turns the attention of the sense organ toward the object,[68] and suitable conditions in the environment as, for example, proper light in the case of sight. In some way the sensible object affects the sense organ, producing a change or modification in it. The change in the sense organ cannot affect the soul, but the soul becomes aware of the modifications and forms an idea of the modification out of its own spiritual substance.

For both Augustine and Plotinus the soul makes images of the bodily passions. Sensation is the awareness in the soul of these images.

This point is important for Augustine, since his theory of knowledge seems to be a representational theory—what the mind or soul perceives are not physical objects but images of the objects. He tells us that the visible object

> produces the form, which is, as it were, its own likeness, which comes to be in the sense, when we perceive anything by seeing. But we do not distinguish, through the same sense, the form of the body which we see, from the form which is produced by it in the sense of him who sees; since the union of the two is so close that there is no room for distinguishing them. But we rationally infer that we could not have sensation at all, unless some similitude of the body seen was wrought in our own sense.[69]

The mind receives incoming messages mediated by the senses. The messages remain outside the mind and images of the messages are formed by the mind.[70] The mind forms an incorporeal likeness of physical objects and then commits this likeness or image to the memory. The mind

has the ability, when it so wills, not only to bring these images out of the storehouse of the memory but also to draw the distinction between the corporeal object outside the mind and the incorporeal likeness (image) within the mind.[71]

Augustine uses two different terms for image. He distinguishes between *phantasia* and *phantasm*—although he does not always use them consistently. *Phantasia* is a simple image received from sensation that is stored in the memory.[72] By *phantasm* he means an arbitrary image of a thing not perceived through the senses but formed in the imagination from other memory images. "For my father I have often seen I know, in one way, or my grandfather I have never seen, another way. The first of these is a *phantasia*, the other *phantasm*. The first I find in my memory, the last in that motion of my mind born of those the memory has. It's one thing to find a *phantasia* in the memory and another to make a *phantasm* out of the memory."[73]

In connection with Augustine's view of images there is a passage that is worth noticing, even though Augustine later modified it in certain important respects. In his seventh epistle Augustine writes of three classes of images. "All these mental images, which you, like many others call fantasies, I think can be most conveniently and most correctly divided into three classes: the first comprises true sense impressions; the second, images of things supposed; the third, of things thought."[74]

Augustine must have recognized the incongruity of a Platonist such as himself speaking of the ideas of reason as images, for he does not speak again of the third class he mentions in this way. However, this passage is important not only because it throws light on Augustine's theory of sensation but also because it contains a clear anticipation of a point later emphasized by Descartes.

Augustine's three types of images bear a remarkable resemblance to Descartes' three classes of ideas—adventitious, factitious, and innate.

> To consider now the ideas (that are strictly so called), some appear to me to be innate, others to be adventitious, that is to say foreign to me and coming from without, and others to be made or invented by me. When I apprehend what a thing is, what a truth is, or what a thought is, I would seem to be holding the power of so doing from no other source than my own nature. On the other hand, when I hear a sound, see the Sun, or sense fire, I have hitherto judged these to proceed from certain things situated outside me. Lastly it appears to me that sirens, hippogriffs and other similar chimeras are my own mental inventions.[75]

Augustine's first class of images (corresponding to Descartes' adventitious ideas) includes images originating in sense experience. In his seventh epistle Augustine is sure that Nebridus—to whom the letter is written—will concede that the mind possesses images of such things as the city of Carthage or the face of a friend only because it has use of the bodily senses. Augustine is convinced that the soul could not form images of corporeal objects if it were deprived of its bodily senses. In support of this he argues that if sense organs were not a necessary condition for this type of image, then a sleeping or insane man might have images more reliable than the man who is awake or sane.[76] Augustine admits that in a strict sense of the word we do not "see" this image; that is, we are usually aware only of the object being perceived. But, he argues, neither when a ring is pressed into wax do we perceive its imprint until it is removed. Still it is obvious that even though we cannot see the image while the ring is still pressed into the wax, there must be an image, since it remains once the ring is removed. Suppose, to take an-

other example, that the ring is impressed in a liquid substance. After the ring is removed, no image is visible, but dare one assume that there was not in some sense an image while the ring was immersed in the liquid? Augustine's point is that when we perceive a sensible object, we are usually not aware of an image but only of the object being perceived. Nevertheless, upon reflection we realize that without some likeness of the object, sensation would have been impossible. Thus, there are some images that the mind could not have without being related in some way to the sense organs.[77]

The second class of images (Descartes' factitious ideas) includes those that originate in the imagination. It is possible, for example, to have an image of a god of Greek mythology or a creature like a centaur or unicorn. Or one can make up images as he teaches or illustrates a truth. Also, it is a common experience that when one is being told a story, he finds in his mind pictures or images of the events being recounted. These images are subject to much more doubt than the images derived from experience. "But who will doubt that those imaginings are much more false than the images of things experienced? It is equally true that the things which we suppose and believe or imagine are utterly and completely false and those which we see or experience are far more true."[78]

The mind can have images of this class which are not dependent upon the senses. Augustine suggests that the mind has an innate power to add to or subtract from the images it receives from the senses. One may have, for example, an image of a crow that is derived from sensation. It is possible to add to that image, however, such characteristics as longer wings and a different color and thus end up with an image of something never perceived. "It is possible for the imagination to alter the data brought in by the senses, and by subtraction, as we said, or by ad-

dition, to produce things which in their totality have been experienced by none of the senses, although parts of them have been experienced in one or another instance."[79] Although one has never actually seen the sea, it is possible to imagine what the sea is like from having seen water in a cup. However, there are exceptions. It is impossible to imagine how strawberries or cherries taste without having experienced their taste. "That is why those who are born blind are unable to answer when they are questioned about light and color: they cannot imagine color because they have never perceived any."[80]

The third class of images (corresponding to Descartes' innate ideas) includes those that originate in reason alone, apart from any use of the senses. Augustine soon stopped discussing this class of ideas under the heading of images. This type of image includes knowledge of the relationships between numbers, musical harmonies, moral standards, and other universals. The reliability of these images, which cannot be pictured, implies that the soul is capable of knowing truth apart from the senses.

Augustine regards sensation as an awareness in the soul of a modification in the body. But all the soul ever reaches is the form in the sense organ, and all the soul is ever aware of is the image that it produces in itself. Augustine believes that an external object is necessary to produce the change in the sense organ, but since all the soul ever knows is an incorporeal representation of this impression, it may be asked how Augustine knows there is an external object. Sister Mary Ann Ida Gannon believes that Augustine could not explain how

> the awareness of a passion in the body, or of the form produced in the presence of that passion, can provide an adequate knowledge of the object which caused it. . . . Augustine, always a realist, constantly appeals to experience for evidence that it is the external body

that is seen, and more than once wonders at the manner in which the form of the external body affects the soul without ever leaving that body. His theory seems effectively to cut off the soul from the object itself.[81]

Later Augustinians went further and asserted that there is no direct relationship between the soul and sensible objects and that, consequently, the objects the soul senses are its own creations. Augustine would not have agreed with this, but his view contains principles that lead logically to such a conclusion. Undoubtedly, Augustine's answer about how we know that our concepts correspond with reality is God.[82] This seems to put him in the company of such men as Descartes and Berkeley, who also were saved from solipsism by God. But there is perhaps a danger of making too much of this problem when it comes to Augustine. As Copleston sees it, Augustine "was not occupied with the question whether the external world really exists or not. He felt no doubt that it exists, though he saw clearly enough that we sometimes make erroneous judgments about it and that testimony is not always reliable, whether it be testimony of our own senses or of other people."[83]

Sense perception posed a number of continuing problems for Augustine—problems that he could never quite resolve. Although his treatment of a sensation is inadequate, it should be remembered that for him the bifurcation between sense perception and the spiritual vision is an unnatural one. Man does have sensations, and he does have the capacity to attain, as a result of prior sense experience, *scientia*.

chapter
five : cogitation

Man has much in common with the beasts. Augustine mentions such things as a physical body, life, sensation, the ability to form images, and the capacity to remember sensations. Things that man has in common with the beasts, Augustine says, belong to the outer man.[1] Capacities that man does not share with the beasts belong to the inner man. Included in the latter class are man's ability to judge, compare, and measure sensations.

Animals can perceive corporeal things through the bodily senses, store images of them in the memory, recall them, and use the memory to seek things that they desire or to shun things that they wish to avoid. However, the beast cannot relate these perceptions and memory images to truth or to the eternal standards as can man. Augustine says that when he recalls a beautiful stone arch he once saw at Carthage, there is more in his mind than simply an image of that arch. "I behold in my mind yet another thing, according to which that work of art pleases me; and whence also, if it displeased me, I should correct it. We judge therefore of those particular things according to that [form of eternal truth] and discern that form by the intuition of the rational mind."[2]

Furthermore, man cannot only retain naturally what he has perceived (a capacity he shares with the beasts), but he can deliberately commit something to memory, and

when things stored in his memory begin to slip away into forgetfulness, he can refresh his memory.

There is, therefore, a crucial distinction between mere sensation and human knowledge of sensible things. The second is a step higher on Augustine's ladder of knowledge. This progression from sensation to *scientia* is well illustrated by Augustine's remarks about the powers of the soul.[3] In *De quantitate animae* he notices seven levels or powers of the soul—animation *(animatio)*, sensation *(sensus)*, ratiocination *(ars)*,[4] virtue or evaluation *(virtus)*, tranquillity *(tranquillitas)*, fixation *(ingressio)*, and contemplation *(contemplatio)*. The powers of animation, sensation, and ratiocination are relevant here.

The first level of the soul is animation (compare Aristotle's vegetative soul). This is the life that the soul by its presence gives to a corporeal body. The power of the soul unifies the various functions of the body, keeps the body from dissolution, and regulates its nourishment.[5] This lowest power is shared by man and other forms of life, including vegetation. The next level is sensation (compare Aristotle's appetitive soul). Man shares this only with animals. Augustine believes that this power of the soul is exhibited not only by the capacity to experience sensations but also by other powers common to both man and animals, such as propagation, protection and care of offspring, and instinct.[6] This power of the soul belongs to the exterior man.

The third level is what Augustine terms *ars* or ratiocination. Only man possesses this power, which can be seen in his ability to make works of art, till the land, build cities, use symbols to communicate, write books, and form governments. "Great are these achievements and distinctively human. Yet, this heritage, common to all rational souls, is shared in by the learned and the unlearned, by the good and the wicked."[7]

Scientia becomes possible on this third level of the soul.

The distinctive features of this level include man's application of universal standards to data provided by the senses and his use of the knowledge for some practical purpose. The question of truth now becomes relevant. Mere sensations are neither true nor false—truth belongs to judgments about the sensations.

Augustine construes knowledge *(scientia)* as a product of both the mind and the world, because, as he writes, "knowledge is brought forth from both, from the knower and the thing known."[8] Mere sensation cannot produce *scientia*, unless the mind passes judgment on the information furnished by the senses. In the process from the object of perception to its image in the mind external bodies act upon the sense organs of the body. Because the soul is always attentive to modifications in the body, it is immediately aware of them and from its own spiritual substance makes an image corresponding to the physical change in the sense organ. Thus, while the mind receives incoming messages mediated by the senses, the messages remain outside the mind and images of them are formed by the mind. The mind forms an incorporeal likeness of physical objects and then commits the likeness or image to the memory. The process has not yet accounted for *scientia*, however. Man attains *scientia* of sensible things through a process that Augustine calls cogitation *(cogitatio)*.

Cogitation is the function of man's mind by which he can arrange, collect, and reassemble sense knowledge stored in the memory. When the stored images are forgotten, "they must be marshalled *(cogenda)* again that they may become known; that is to say, they must be collected *(colligenda)*, as it were, from their dispersion; whence we have the word *cogitare*."[9] The same point is made in *De Trinitate:* "Like one who is skilled in many branches of learning: the things which he knows are contained in his memory, but nothing thereof is in the sight

of his mind except that of which he is conceiving; while all the rest are stored up in a kind of secret knowledge, which is called memory."[10]

Cogitantis is dependent upon prior sense perceptions that are stored in the memory which the mind may act upon.[11]

Since *cogitatio* is related to the ability of man's mind to act upon sense images, the various powers or faculties of the soul must be understood. *Anima* is not a faculty of the soul; the term refers to the soul itself. Augustine uses *anima* to refer to man's vital principle, that which gives life to the body.[12] In this sense both men and animals have souls.[13] Occasionally, however, Augustine uses a different term when he speaks particularly of the human soul—*animus*.[14] Thus, *animus*, which is sometimes used interchangeably with *mens* or mind,[15] means more than *anima*, because it refers to man's soul not only as the principle of life but also as the basis of reason.[16]

Augustine uses *spiritus* in two distinct senses.[17] First, he sometimes uses it in the usual Scriptural sense as referring to the rational part of man's soul.[18] Thus, while the soul is "the life whereby we are united with the body," spirit is a "certain rational portion of" the soul.[19] Given this meaning, *spiritus* and *mens* can be used interchangeably.[20]

However, Augustine writes, we can also speak "of a spirit in man distinct from the mind, to which spirit belongs the images that are formed after the likenesses of bodies."[21] Augustine explains that in this sense *spiritus* is a power of the soul lower than *mens* (mind) but higher than life *(anima)* in which images or likenesses of corporeal things are expressed.[22]

Augustine uses the term *mens* in agreement with certain Latin writers to "distinguish that which excells in man and is not in the beast, from the soul *(anima)*, which is in the beast as well."[23] *Mens* is the part of *animus* (the

substantial, rational human soul) that is concerned with God and intelligible things. *Mens* is superior to the senses, since it judges their reports,[24] but it is inferior to the divine ideas, since they in a sense rule the mind.[25]

Augustine regards the mind as the faculty of the soul that includes the soul's capacities of reason and intellect.[26] "If reason and mind are different things we at least agree that only mind can make use of reason. Hence it is concluded that he who has reason cannot lack mind."[27] This means that the possession of a mind is a necessary condition for the exercise of reason, and, although the text does not mention the fact, for the intellect as well. Even in men who fail to make use of reason (for example, fools), there is still evidence that they possess minds.

Augustine also uses *ratio* in more than one sense. "Reason is a mental operation capable of distinguishing and connecting the things that are learned."[28] *Ratio*, then, is sometimes used to refer to the power man has to analyze and synthesize data to find relevant connections. It is the capacity of *mens* to move from one item of knowledge to another.

Augustine also regards reason as the contemplation of truth. It is, in the words of the *Soliloquies*, "the mind's act of looking."[29] When *ratio* is used with this meaning, it is related to *mens* as sight is to the eye. As the mere possession of eyes is not enough to guarantee sight, so too the mind must look if it is to see truth.

Finally, Augustine uses *ratio* to refer to the truth that the mind beholds.[30] Although Augustine himself does not mention the fact, these three uses of *ratio* do constitute a kind of trinity. *Ratio* can mean either the mind's power to know, the exercise of that power, or the object of the power, the *rationes aeternae*.

He further differentiates *ratio* as a permanent faculty of the mind from *ratiocinatio*, the use of that faculty.

Ratio is always inherent in a sound mind,[31] but a mind need not constantly carry on the process of reasoning (*ratiocinatio*).[32] "Reason (ratio), you might say, is the sight of the mind, but reasoning is reason's search, that is, the actual moving of the sight of the mind over the things that are to be seen. Hence, by reasoning, we search; by reason we see."[33]

Augustine distinguished between the *ratio superior* and *ratio inferior*, the higher and lower reasons. These two aspects of the same mind have different objects, methods, ends, and results. The object of the lower reason is the temporal world of particulars;[34] its method is investigation; its end is action; and its result is *scientia*. The object of the higher reason is the eternal world of the forms; its method is contemplation; its end is happiness; and its result is *sapientia*. It is especially important that for Augustine *ratio superior* and *intellectus* refer to the same faculty.

Intellectus is a faculty of the mind above reason, specifically above *ratio inferior*. It is that part of the soul illumined by the divine light.

> For the understanding (intellectus) is not something other than the soul, but a thing of the soul: as the eye is a thing of the flesh, yet it alone enjoys the light; and the other fleshly members may be steeped in light, but they cannot feel the light: the eye alone is both bathed in it and enjoys it. Thus in our soul there is something called the understanding (*intellectus*). This something of the soul, which is called understanding and mind (mens) is enlightened by the higher light. Now that higher light by which the human mind is enlightened, is God.[35]

This argument implies that while man's mind is illumined by the divine light and thus enabled to know, man only becomes aware of this light through his under-

standing. *Intellectus* is the eye by which the mind sees the intelligible world.[36] Because of this Augustine regards the intellect as the most eminent faculty in man.[37]

Cogitatio could not take place without the memory. The knowledge it actualizes must first be present in the memory. Cogitation is described as the product of three things—the memory, the internal vision, and the will.[38] The memory is the most complicated of these notions and requires an extended discussion.

The first step that must be taken in approaching this aspect of Augustine's thought is to put aside our ordinary understanding of memory. For Augustine the term "memory" includes more than is usually attributed to it. He understands memory as the storehouse of all that is potential or latent within the mind. The memory contains not only images of past experiences but also, in a sense that requires careful explanation, innate ideas that correspond to the eternal forms. This helps to explain Augustine's paradoxical view that thinking, learning, and remembering are all the same.[39]

In the memory are stored images of things perceived through the senses.[40] The past is remembered as the images are brought into the consciousness. The memory is also a storehouse for recollections of our own states of consciousness. "There also do I meet with myself, and recall myself—what, when or where I did a thing, and how I was affected when I did it."[41] By means of memory I can remember that I remembered.[42] Without memory it is clear that the past would be closed and forgotten.

But memory also plays a part in present sensation. For example, when I hear a word of more than one syllable, I must remember the beginning until I hear the end. Unless sensations can be tied together in some way, it is difficult to see how the senses could provide any basis for *scientia*.

If our knowledge of past and present experience depends

upon the memory, so must our anticipation of future experience. Augustine analyzes some of the phrases often used to refer to anticipations of the future, for example, "I will do this or that," "Oh that this or that might come to pass," or "God avert this or that!" He explains, "Thus, I speak to myself; and when I speak, the images of all I speak about are present, out of the same treasury of memory; nor could I say anything at all about them were the images absent."[43] His point seems to be this: One cannot speak meaningfully about the future unless the things anticipated have some relation to things already experienced. For example, many Christians have believed that the life to come will be completely different from life as it is now known. Unless Heaven is described in terms of things experienced in this life, however, unless Heaven is spoken of as a city of gold or eternal mansions or even a wedding feast, it will be completely unintelligible.

The memory is a storehouse for thoughts of the eternal truths. This point is extremely important to Augustine's theory of knowledge. *Scientia* is possible only because man can judge sensible things according to eternal standards.[44]

Augustine is confronted by a dilemma. Although it is true that the eternal reasons must be above man's mind (or else they would not be unchangeable), it is also the case that "unless something of our own were subjoined to them (the reasons), we should not be able to employ them as our measures by which to judge of corporeal things."[45] In other words, if the divine ideas are not distinct from man's mind, they are not immutable, but, on the other hand, if they are not "subjoined" to the mind, they cannot be used as standards of judgment. This may involve the most crucial problem that Augustine's theory of knowledge has to face—the difficulty of relating the human (and mutable) aspect of knowledge to the divine (immutable) aspect. Gilson, who believes Augustinism

cannot solve the problem, states it this way: "Truth [for Augustine] is too good for man. As soon as there is truth, there is God. How then can truth become ours? As long as it is God's truth, it is unchangeable and necessary, i.e., truth itself. As soon as it is created in us, it must be changeable, temporal and contingent, like the intellect which receives it. In this case, is it still the truth?"[46]

It is too soon to see if Gilson's question has an answer. However, it is clear that there is no simple answer. It is possible, though, that Augustine's point about the memory's being a repository of thoughts of the divine ideas may, when coupled with his arguments about divine illumination, enable us to arrive at a solution.

There are two important passages in which Augustine talks about the memory's relation to necessary truth. In the *Confessions* he writes, "The memory contains also the reasons [*i.e.*, the forms] and innumerable laws of numbers and dimensions, none of which has any sense of the body impressed."[47] The text implies that the forms and laws are present in the memory as latent or virtual truth. They are present not necessarily as objects of thought but as predispositions of the mind to think in certain ways. The memory contains thoughts or notions of the forms even when they are not objects of thought. It is clear that Augustine would have disagreed with Locke who held that the mind can have ideas only when it is conscious of them. Although it may be misleading to use Kantian terminology when talking about Augustine, there is a strong temptation to describe these laws as *a priori* forms of thought.[48]

In the second passage Augustine mentions the eternal reasons and adds that very few men are able to attain them with the eye of the mind. Even when they are known as much as possible, "he himself who attains to them does not abide in them, but is as it were repelled by the rebounding of the eye itself of the mind, and so

there comes to be a transitory thought of a thing not transitory. And yet this transient thought is committed to the memory . . . that the mind . . . may be able to return thither again."[49]

There are three ways in which this text may be related to the previously quoted one from the *Confessions*. First, they could be regarded as contradictory, *i.e.*, the *Confessions* text states that the reasons are in the memory, while the *De Trinitate* text asserts that they are not. However, the charge that they are incompatible is based upon a superficial reading of the *De Trinitate* text. A careful reading suggests other views. A second possibility is that the *De Trinitate* text may explain how the eternal laws and ideas are in the memory of man. Augustine may be drawing an analogy between intellection and sensation. Just as the images of sensible things, seen by the senses, are stored in the memory, man sees with the eye of his mind the divine ideas. But since he is unable to dwell with them for any length of time, thoughts of the ideas are committed to his memory. This explanation is plausible. It is also possible that the text in *De Trinitate* only uses a metaphor to illustrate what would otherwise be an unexplainable situation. For example, some interpreters of Plato believe that his discussion in the *Phaedo* in which he argues that the souls have beheld the forms in another existence should not be taken literally. On this view, Plato could find no other explanation of how man knows *a priori* truth so he developed this illustration, which should be regarded in the same class as the myth of the cave in *The Republic*. Thus, it is possible that Augustine, finding the existence of necessary truth in man's mind too difficult to explain in any other way, also resorts to a metaphor. It is still possible that the *a priori* forms of thought belong to man's mind in some nonacquired sense. Augustine does believe that the memory contains thoughts or notions of the eternal reasons. One of his reasons for

this is his belief that they are in man's mind even when they are not the objects of thought.

The memory contains images of things perceived, and it retains acquired skills, such as skill in argumentation and the answers to questions and passages of great literature.[50] There is nothing new in attributing these powers to the memory. However, Augustine does refer what is sometimes called dispositional knowledge to the memory.[51] Man knows many things, even though he may not always be thinking of them. For example, a musician may know a piece of music, even though he is not thinking of it at a particular moment. The proof that he knows it is exhibited when he reproduces it—by playing the music, singing it, or stating some fact about it. "And hence we are warned that we have a kind of knowledge of certain things stored up in the recesses of the mind, and that this, when it is thought of, as it were, steps forth in public, and is placed as if openly in the sight of the mind."[52]

Augustine develops a further aspect of the virtual knowledge that resides in the memory when he discusses the relationship between memory and the knowledge of God and the blessed life.[53] He first asserts that memory cannot provide the knowledge of God. In spite of the powers of the memory, he writes, "I will pass even beyond this power of mine which is called memory—I will pass beyond it, that I may proceed to Thee, O Thou sweet Light."[54] Then he asks, "But where shall I find thee? If I find Thee not without memory, then am I unmindful of Thee. And how now shall I find Thee, if I do not remember Thee?"[55] His point is, how can I seek God and the happy life unless I know what it is that I am looking for. How can I seek unless I have in some way known the objects of my search, for if I do not know them, I will not know when I have found them. Since all men seek the blessed life, it is in some way in the

memory? "For did we not know it, we should not live it. . . . It is then known to all, and could they with one voice be asked whether they wished to be happy, without doubt they would all answer that they would. And this could not be unless the thing itself, of which it is the name, were retained in their memory."[56]

How can the blessed life be retained in the memory? Augustine considers four possible answers: First, is the presence of the blessed life in the memory similar to the way in which one remembers having seen the city of Carthage? No, for the blessed life is not corporeal and cannot be seen by the physical eye.[57]

Second, is it analogous to the way in which we remember numbers? No, for he who has numbers does not seek further. Although we may have the blessed life in our minds, we realize that we do not yet possess it, and we continue to search.[58]

Third, is our remembrance of the blessed life like our remembrance of eloquence? This seems at first a more promising analogy, because eloquence can be remembered by those who do not possess it and yet desire it. However, here again the analogy is inadequate, because we perceive eloquence by the bodily senses.

Fourth, can it be similar to our remembrance of joy? Augustine finds this analogy encouraging. We can remember joy even while sad, just as we can have some awareness of what the blessed life is while miserable. Furthermore, joy, unlike eloquence, is not perceived by the physical senses. "Where and when, then, did I experience my happy (i.e., blessed) life, that I should call it to mind, and love and long for it. . . . Is it, perchance, that as one joys in this, and another in that, so do all men agree in their wish for happiness, as they would agree, were they asked, in wishing to have joy—and this joy they call a happy life?"[59]

Men know what it is to experience joy, and the attain-

ment of joy is a universal goal. Because men have experienced joy, they recognize what is meant when the happy life is mentioned.

It is now possible to look at some of the most important passages in which Augustine explains the passage from *sentientis* to *cogitantis*. His discussion leaves a number of gaps that one might wish he had filled, but he says enough to enable us to grasp the essential points.

In section II, 3 to II, 6 of *De libero arbitrio* Augustine engages in one of his favorite pastimes—the discovering of hierarchies of knowledge and of being. Augustine here distinguishes between the object of sensation (for example, the color red), the sense organ (the eye), the interior sense in man's soul, and finally man's reason, which dominates all. The role of the interior sense and the general transition that takes place among these various entities should be examined.

In one way or another corporeal objects produce an impression on the bodily sense organ. Augustine believes that something more happens. When the color that is perceived affects the sense organ, the "sense of sight in the eyes" then reports "to the interior sense."[60] The interior sense then reports directly to the reason. "There is a kind of interior sense to which the ordinary senses refer everything. . . . This sense can be called neither sight nor hearing nor smell nor taste nor touch, but must be some other sense which presides over all the others alike. While we comprehend this (sense) by reason, as I said, still we cannot call it reason, since clearly the beasts have it too."[61] This interior sense perceives not only the data from the senses but also the senses themselves. It distinguishes which things belong to which sense and which things belong to several senses.[62]

Unless the data from the physical senses goes beyond the interior sense, however, there can be no knowledge. Augustine cannot believe that animals understand that

the light they perceive is perceived by their eyes and not their ears. Such knowledge depends upon an intelligence not found in brutes.[63] Though the interior sense is able to perceive both the corporeal objects perceived by the bodily senses as well as the bodily sense, it is not able to judge what it perceives according to rational standards. Because reason judges both the senses and the interior sense, it is superior to both.[64]

Since there are no references to the interior sense in Augustine's later writings, he may have come to believe that he did not need this notion. Nevertheless, this passage is significant because of its expression of two points that Augustine recognized early in his philosophic development. First, the information furnished by the senses does not become knowledge until it is judged by the reason. Secondly, in tracing the passage from sensation to the reason Augustine recognizes the need for some intermediate step—the process of sense perception is too complicated simply to allow that information from the senses is relayed immediately to reason. To fill this gap Augustine refers to the interior sense, whose function is not completely clear to him. In later writings the gap will be filled by what he calls the memory.

In *De Trinitate* XI, 2-3 Augustine searches for analogies of the triunity of God. He first discusses what he calls the trinity of the outer man, *i.e.*, the external object, the act of seeing, and the attention of the mind.[65] Without some external object to sense there can be no sensation. But Augustine also speaks of *visio*, which is the sense informed by the external object. *Visio*, illustrated by the act of seeing, is the union of sense and external object. Finally, Augustine mentions *intentio*. If sense perception is to take place, the will of the mind must direct the sense organ to the object and keep the mind's attention focused on the object. Though all three aspects of the trinity of the outer man are important, Augustine stresses

the significance of *intentio*. It is possible to have objects that can be perceived as well as perfectly healthy sense organs and still not perceive. The attention of the mind must be fixed on the object. The result of sense perception is an image that is stored in the memory. What happens to this image is explained by what Augustine calls the trinity of the inner man.

The cooperation of the trinity of the outer man produces the trinity of the inner man, *i.e.*, the image in the memory, the internal vision, and the will. From the cooperation of this trinity comes *cogitatio*.[66]

> Since even if the form of the body, which was corporeally perceived, be withdrawn, its likeness remains in the memory, to which the will may again direct its eye, so as to be formed then from within, as the sense was formed from without by the presentation of the sensible body. And so that trinity is produced from memory, from internal vision, and from the will which unites both. And when these three things are combined into one, from that combination itself they are called conception (*cogitatio*).[67]

Even though the images of things perceived may be contained in the memory, the mind must decide whether to use them or to refer them to something else. When images of past experiences just happen to flash into the consciousness, these cannot be considered instances in which *cogitatio* occurs. Cogitation takes place only when the mind consciously and deliberately focuses its eye on certain images. "As the will applies this sense to the bodily object, so it applies the memory to the sense, and the eye of the mind of the concipient to the memory. But that which harmonizes those things and unites them, itself also disjoins and separates them, that is, the will."[68]

But what is this "eye of the mind" that Augustine mentions? He is struggling for words to describe what he believes must be the case, and his phrase is clearly

metaphorical. The most plausible answer refers the phrase back to Augustine's other point that *ratio* is the sight of the mind,[69] the mind's act of seeing. This interpretation has at least one thing in its favor. It explains how Augustine can speak of both the *ratio* and *intellectus* as the eye of the mind. *Intellectus,* or the higher reason, is the eye by which the mind sees the intelligible world and which makes *sapientia* possible. The *ratio inferior* is the eye by which the mind sees sense images stored in the memory and which makes *scientia* possible.

In the important passage *De Trinitate* XI, 9, 16 Augustine notes four steps in the transition from sensation to rational knowledge or, in Augustine's terminology, from the bodily species[70] or form to the species in the intuition. First, there is the species of the external body, which can be termed the corporeal species. This is simply the object as it is in itself. Second, the corporeal species produces a sensible species, which is the way the object appears for the sense. He remarks that "we could not have sensation at all, unless some similitude of the body seen was wrought in our own sense."[71] That is, some likeness of the object is impressed on the sense organ.[72] Third, the sensible species produces a likeness in the memory. This step accounts for our present perception of objects. Fourth, this last likeness that is stored in the memory produces the image that is perceived in the act of remembering.

The first two steps produce corporeal vision or *sentientis*. The last two steps account for spiritual vision or *cogitantis*. A likeness of the sensible object is impressed on the sense organ producing a physical change in that organ. The soul becomes aware of the modification in the body and produces a corresponding image out of its own substance. This image is received by the memory and produces either the present perception of the object or the memory of it.

chapter
    six : intellection,
            man's knowledge
            of the
            forms

T HE question of how man knows the *rationes
aeternae* or divine ideas may be the most important and
the most difficult problem in Augustine's theory of
knowledge. A knowledge of the forms is what makes
both *scientia* and *sapientia* possible. Therefore, if we are
to see the grounds that make knowledge and wisdom
possible, Augustine must provide an adequate explanation to the question of how man becomes acquainted with
the eternal standards of truth.

The forms are the eternal, immutable truths (corresponding to Plato's forms) that exist in the mind of
God. Augustine does not allow the complete separation
of the intellectual and physical worlds that Plato apparently did. Instead, all created reality for Augustine
exists in two modes—the physical and the intelligible
(the divine mind).[1]

To be sure, God is truth, but Augustine also speaks of
ontological truth that resides in created reality. Augustine
would not agree with much of modern philosophy that
tends to restrict truth to a quality of propositions; nor
would he concur with the tendency to regard logical

principles as purely formal statements. Just as all of God's creation is good, so all of reality partakes of truth in varying degrees. Inasmuch as creatures embody or exemplify the form or pattern in the mind of God, they possess ontological truth. The principles of logic are not empty statements devoid of any significant content. "The true nature of logical conclusions has not been arranged by men; rather they studied and took notice of it so that they might be able to learn or to teach it. It is perpetual in the order of things and divinely ordained."[2] Augustine sees no clear distinction between the real order and the logical order. The truth of such a proposition as three plus two equals five does not consist simply in the mental act of making this judgment; rather, its truth lies in the eternal reality which makes the judgment true.

One important consequence of the close relationship that Augustine sees between intellectual and ontological truth is that there is no room for any unknowable *ding an sich*. Reality is knowable because it was created by God after the pattern of the divine ideas. Augustine's next step must be to show that God also created man's mind so that he can know both the *rationes aeternae* and the physical world patterned after these forms.

How then does Augustine explain man's knowledge of the forms? The first difficulty in answering this concerns the great disparity between the nature of man's mind and the nature of the forms. While man's mind is mutable and finite, the eternal truths are necessary and immutable. If Augustine is to provide an adequate explanation of man's knowledge of the forms—and show the conditions under which man's knowledge of anything is possible—he must find some way of relating the apparent contraries.

Augustine rejects several possible answers. One is the notion that the forms are acquired by sense experience. In *De vera religione* Augustine writes, "True equality and similitude, true and primal unity, are not perceived by the

eye of the flesh or by any bodily sense, but are known by the mind."[3] To borrow a term from Kant, Augustine regards man's knowledge of the forms as *a priori*, or independent of experience. He supports the claim with some interesting arguments in *De libero arbitrio*, where he rejects the possibility of an empirical basis for mathematics.

First he points out that the principles of mathematics are the same for all reasoning men. The truths of mathematics are discovered, not invented by men. Although some find mathematics easy and others find it difficult, "the science (of numbers) itself remains the same for everybody who can learn. . . . If anyone makes a mistake in numbers the science itself is not at fault. It remains true and entire."[4]

Then Augustine considers the possible reply that "numbers make their impression on our minds not in their own right but rather as images of visible things (and) spring from our contacts by bodily sense with corporeal objects."[5] Augustine has Evodius reply that even if numbers themselves are perceived by the senses, sense experience cannot perceive the relations that exist between numbers nor the operations that can be performed on numbers. Furthermore, the senses can only report states of affairs that fluctuate and change. For example, one might perceive the sun, the stars, or the earth, but he cannot know on the basis of these perceptions how long they will last. However, seven plus three equals ten not just today but always. Seven and three have never equaled any other sum, and they never will. Thus, once again the science of numbers has been shown to be independent of sensation.

Augustine is not yet finished with his case. He shows that all numbers are multiples of the number one. However, the notion of unity cannot be derived from experience. "Whoever thinks with exactitude of unity will certainly discover that it cannot be perceived by the senses. What-

ever comes into contact with a bodily sense is proved to be not one but many, for it is corporeal and therefore has innumerable parts."[6]

That is, our bodily senses can only bring us into contact with corporeal things, and physical things, no matter how small they are, have innumerable or least multiple parts. If nothing else one can distinguish the left side from the right side of the object or the top from the bottom. Because every corporeal thing has parts, it cannot be considered a true and absolute unity. In order to know that no body is a unity, which is tantamount to admitting that the notion of unity cannot be derived from the senses, one still must have some idea of what unity is. "If I did not know what unity is, I could not count the plurality of parts in a body. However I have come to know unity, I have not learned it from the bodily senses, for by them I can know only corporeal objects, and none of them, as we have proved is a true unity."[7] Moreover, if unity is not perceived through the senses, neither is any other number, because all numbers are multiples of one.

One more argument in this context is especially worth noting because it anticipates a point that occurs much later in the writings of David Hume. Augustine notices that in constructing number series we are certain that numbers will maintain the same relationships as ratios, even though we do not carry on the series.

> And throughout the numerical series you will find the same role holds good from first to last. The double of any number is found to be exactly as far from that number as it is from the beginning of the series. How do we find this changeless, firm and unbroken rule persisting throughout the numerical series? No bodily sense makes contact with all numbers, for they are innumerable. How do we know that this rule holds throughout? How can any phantasy or phantasm [i.e., sense-image] yield such certain truth about numbers which are innumerable?[8]

In other words, it is impossible to justify on empirical grounds the knowledge we have about the properties of number series. The number series can always be continued beyond our experience, yet we feel justified in making assertions about the properties of these series even though our conclusions clearly go beyond our empirical evidence. Augustine's remarks about mathematics seems to confront him with a problem similar to the one that David Hume raised about causation. Hume showed that all judgments about causation go beyond the empirical data. Since such judgments are also unrelated to relations of ideas, Hume concluded that neither reason nor experience can justify any judgment of the form "x causes y." Hume was not bothered by this problem insofar as it relates to mathematics. He also admitted that mathematics could not be based upon experience, but he then proceeded to divorce completely the truths of mathematics from matters of fact. Augustine would have rejected Hume's separation of mathematical truth from ontology. Augustine, though aware that mathematical truths could not be justified on empirical grounds, rejected the kind of solution that the twentieth-century positivists (following Hume) have accepted—the regarding of mathematical truths as analytic or tautological statements that are true solely by virtue of their assigned meanings.

Mathematics confronted Augustine with the same type of problem that Hume faced in justifying judgments about causation. Although Augustine likely was not as aware of this problem as Kant, one can find nonetheless some interesting anticipations of Kant in this aspect of Augustine's theory of knowledge. Regardless of how important Augustine thought the problem to be, he was still searching for the grounds that make mathematics possible. What was his answer? Unfortunately, he states it in only one sentence. "We must know this [the truth of mathematical statements that go beyond experience]

by the inner light, of which bodily sense knows nothing."[9] Man's knowledge of necessary truth is accounted for by his doctrine of illumination. This theory is discussed more fully in several of his later works. Augustine argues then that our knowledge of the forms is independent of experience. An important illustration of this thesis can be seen in his remarks about our knowledge of mathematical truths.

Augustine argues in a similar way about the principles of geometry. It seems to him that "it would be easier to sail on dry land than to learn geometry by the senses."[10] The principles of ethics also are universal and are known by the reason.

> Again, I believe you do not deny that men should strive after wisdom. You admit that this is true? . . . Here is another truth which is one and common to all who know it, though each one sees it with his own mind and not with mine or yours or any other man's. . . . Again, take such propositions as these: Man ought to live justly; the worse ought to be subjected to the better; like is to be compared with like; each man should be given his due. . . . Could anyone claim truths of that kind as his own private truths, seeing they are unchangeably present for all to contemplate who have the capacity to contemplate them?[11]

Thus, Augustine holds that the eternal truths are absolute and unchanging and therefore have an objective existence independent of the varying sensations, feelings, and wishes of men.[12] Because the reports of the senses are variable, mutable, often deceptive, and unreliable, Augustine believes that sensation is unable to account for our knowledge of ideas that are certain, necessary, and immutable.

Augustine also rejected the view that the forms are acquired through Platonic recollection. In the *Phaedo* Plato thought that man's knowledge of the forms is a result of

his having seen them in an existence prior to birth. Plato regarded all human knowledge as a kind of recollection or reminiscence of what the soul had known in a previous existence.[13]

Because of the influence that the Platonists had on Augustine, he must have considered this view as a possible explanation of how man attains a knowledge of the forms. Augustine, in fact, uses the term "recollection" not only in the years immediately after his conversion[14] but even in the writings of his more mature years.[15]

It may be impossible to settle the question of whether Augustine during the first few years after his conversion (A.D. 387-389) actually believed in the preexistence of the soul. A more significant point is the position he held after his thought had matured, and on this subject the evidence is more conclusive. For example, in his *Retractiones* Augustine comments on the passage from *De quantitate animae* which states that learning is nothing more than remembering.

> My statement that learning is simply remembering and recalling is not to be taken as if I approved the doctrine that the soul had sometimes existed in another body, here or elsewhere, or in its own body or out of it. . . . Surely the soul does not bring with it all the arts nor does it possess them in the same way. For, as regards the arts that pertain to the senses of the body— many branches of medicine and all of astrology—unless a man learns them, he cannot say that he has them. But, these arts which pertain to the understanding alone, he masters for the reason I mentioned, when he has been wisely questioned and reminded either by himself or another, and thus brings forth the right answer.[16]

Augustine makes several important points in this passage. First, he asserts that when he wrote the passage (the text in *De quantitate animae* 20, 34), he did not intend for it to teach the preexistence of the soul. Second, he

stresses the importance of the many branches of learning that depend upon sense experience. He rejects the possibility that a science such as astronomy can be learned or understood apart from any reliance upon sensation. One must at least observe the positions of the stars. Finally and perhaps most important, his *Retractions*—in spite of Augustine's rejection of preexistence—continue to advance the thesis that learning is a kind of remembering. This suggests that in his later writings at least Augustine uses the notion of reminiscence somewhat differently than Plato's concept, which requires a belief in the soul's preexistence. But if this is so, and there seems to be no other alternative open, how does Augustine's theory differ from the Platonic doctrine?

One text that may hold the answer is in the twelfth book of *De Trinitate*.[17] Here Augustine refers to Plato's famous argument in the *Meno* where Socrates elicits geometric truth from an unlettered slave boy. Plato has Socrates conclude that because the boy never learned the truth in this life, it must have been present in his mind from birth. Augustine counters that even if Plato's argument does prove that the slave boy was remembering truths learned in another existence, it does not prove that everyone would have been able to answer so successfully. "For not everyone was a geometrician in the former life, since geometricians are so few among men that scarcely one can be found anywhere." Furthermore, Augustine argues, recollection in the sense of remembering the past is inadequate because this theory cannot possibly account for the things we learn through the senses.[18] The fact that at this moment I am reading words from a page or watching leaves fall to the ground is hardly something that I remember seeing in a past life.

Augustine's theory of recollection, then, is not a remembering of the past. It is, on the contrary, a remembering of the *present*. "When even untrained persons, suit-

ably questioned, are able to return correct answers about some of the arts, a more credible reason is that they have according to their natural capacity the presence of the light of eternal reason. Hence they catch a glimpse of immutable truth. The reason is not that they once knew it and have forgotten, as Plato and others like him have thought."[19]

Augustine can speak of recollection as a remembering of the present because the truth is always available to us in the sense that Christ will make it available if we are attentive to it. To know truth is to remember now, in the present, the continuous presence of God's light within us. Augustine's theory of memory—that learning, thinking, and remembering are essentially the same—helps in understanding this point. Inasmuch as Augustine regards the memory as the storehouse of virtual knowledge, there is an important link between his doctrine of memory and his teaching about illumination. Man does not remember truths learned in some previous existence but actualizes latent or virtual knowledge of necessary truth that has been stored in what Augustine calls the memory. This notion of recollection and his views about the *a priori* (nonempirical) ground of necessary truth are closely related to Augustine's doctrine of divine illumination.

If man does not acquire his knowledge of the forms through sense experience or through Platonic recollection, does it come through teaching? In his treatise *De magistro* Augustine admits that the soul's ideas appear to have their origin in things outside the soul. This certainly seems true in the case of teaching, where the pupil appears not to be the source of the ideas he learns but instead seems to receive them from his teacher. However, Augustine shows in a long and circuitous argument that this is not necessarily the case. Augustine's argument proceeds in dialectical fashion and is sometimes difficult

to follow, for during its course he often asserts with great certainty statements that are later denied with equal confidence. For example, the conclusion of the first part of *De magistro* is that nothing can be taught without signs; the second part of the dialogue concludes with the claim that nothing can be taught with signs. It must be remembered that Augustine was well schooled in the art of rhetoric and the science of arguing dialectically. This method, which is illustrated in the writings of Parmenides and Zeno and especially in the second part of Plato's *Parmenides,* begins with the acceptance of the very position one is trying to refute. By showing that this position leads to a contradiction or absurdity, one can effectively demonstrate the truth of the opposite position. Thus, Augustine's apparently contradictory conclusions (namely, that nothing can be taught without signs and that nothing can be taught with signs) are part of an involved reductio ad absurdum argument. Augustine's special concern in *De magistro* is not to establish or attack any theory of signs but to show that another position, namely, the view that truth can be communicated through teaching, leads to a contradiction and must therefore be false. Since there is no necessary relationship between symbols (either written or spoken) and thought, the possession of ideas does not depend upon their communication through signs.

Augustine draws a number of distinctions in the first half of *De magistro.* He distinguishes between signs *(signa)* and that which they signify *(signifibilia)*.[20] He shows that though words are signs, not all signs are words.[21] To be more specific, *signa* "signifies absolutely everything by means of which anything is signified," and words are signs "uttered by the articulate voice."[22] If Augustine's position is to make any sense, this last statement should not be taken literally. Augustine probably was trying to distinguish between signs and symbols. A sign is anything

that signifies or stands for something else, for example, dense black clouds are a sign of rain and falling leaves a sign of approaching winter. A symbol (what Augustine calls *verbum*) is an artificial human sign expressed in speaking or writing. While all symbols are signs, not all signs are symbols. Thus when Augustine defines a word as a sign uttered by the articulate voice, he should not be understood as excluding the written word from the class of *verbum*.

He then draws a further distinction between word and noun *(nomen)*. As *signa* is the genus of *verbum*, *nomen* is a species of *verbum*.[23] When Augustine speaks of a noun, he has in mind a word that names something. His examples of words that are nouns include "Romulus," "Rome," "virtue," and "river." In one sense conjunctions such as *et, que, at,* and *atque* are not nouns.[24] However, there is another sense in which "word in general means just as much as noun in general. For our reasoning taught us that all parts of speech are also nouns; for pronouns can be added to them, and it can be said of all that they name something."[25] His meaning here is not immediately clear, but his point can be clarified by comparing it to the distinction made in logic between using a word and mentioning it. For example, it would be difficult to confuse the man Pelagius and his name, but it is easy to get confused when we want to mention (and not use) his name. The following statements are an illustration,

(1) Pelagius is a heretic.
(2) "Pelagius" has eight letters.

In sentence (1) the name "Pelagius" is being used, and in sentence (2) it is being mentioned. If this distinction is ignored as in the following sentences, which are all false, much confusion can arise.

(3) Pelagius has eight letters.
(4) "Pelagius" is a heretic.

Sentence (3) is false because it asserts that the man Pelagius has eight letters, and sentence (4) means that the word "Pelagius" is a heretic.

Augustine holds that there are two ways of understanding the term "noun." Sometimes it is used to signify a part of speech. In this sense conjunctions such as *que* and *et* cannot be considered nouns; that is, when *que* and *et* are used in sentences, they cannot be nouns. When the same words are mentioned, however, they become nouns, inasmuch as they are now the names of certain Latin conjunctions.[26]

Augustine qualifies all this by writing, "But although *word (verbum)* and *noun (nomen)* mean just the same amount because all things which are words are also names, yet they do not mean the same thing. It was argued, and with sufficient reason, that things are called words for one reason and nouns for another, since the former were found to be impressed on the vibration of the ear, but the latter on the memory of the mind."[27]

Although there is a sense in which "word" and "noun" may have the same denotation (in the sense that the same set of symbols can be both a word and a name), they have different connotations. "Word" means *(connotes)* an artificial sign, and "noun" or "name" connotes a sign impressed on the memory of a rational being.

His most important argument in the first part of *De magistro* concerns his claim that nothing can be learned without signs. At first it might seem possible that some things, such as the meaning of the word "wall," can be explained without using other signs. The deaf communicate without words by using gestures to indicate such things as corporeal objects, sounds, and tastes. But, Augustine says, while it is true that the deaf may not use words to communicate, the gestures they make are still signs.[28] A wall itself is a *signifibilia* and not a *signa*, but the act of pointing to a wall in order to explain the

meaning of "wall" is a sign.[29] Augustine notes another problem in the apparent fact that certain actions can be explained without using any sign. For example, it appears that one could explain the meaning of the word "walk" by simply doing the thing named. Augustine finds this inadequate also. He replies, "If I, knowing absolutely nothing of the meaning of the word, should ask you while you are in the act of walking what walking is, how would you teach me?"[30] Adeodatus answers that he would walk more quickly, thereby redirecting the attention of the observer to his action. Augustine finds this no better a solution, for how could the student distinguish between walking and hurrying or between walking and taking five steps? If the act of walking should signify in some way the meaning of "walk," then that act itself is a sign. Should the act not be sufficient to explain the meaning of the term, some additional sign would then have to be given if there is to be any communication about the subject at hand. With arguments such as these Augustine reasons that signs are indispensable in teaching or communicating. Some of Augustine's reasoning to support the claim that nothing can be learned without signs has been considered. How, then, does he support his counterclaim in the second part of De magistro that perhaps nothing is learned through signs?

First, he argues that words are not necessary for the communication of ideas. For example, an Epicurean who denies the immortality of the soul could conceivably recite arguments in favor of the doctrine that would convince his pupils. The pupils who do believe will regard the arguments as valid, and the teacher who uttered the words will not. How can the Epicurean be said to teach what he does not know? And more to the point, what does this example do to the theory under consideration? The teacher uses the same words that his pupils hear, yet both understand something different by them.[31]

Second, he teaches that there is no necessary connection between what the mind knows and the words that express its ideas. We are all familiar with the situation in which one person attempts unsuccessfully to get others to agree with his ideas. In Augustine's judgment this illustrates that men are not passive receptors of ideas expressed through words. On the contrary, men often judge with discrimination what they read or hear.[32]

Third, he suggests that there is no necessary connection between a given set of symbols and some meaning. He refers to the familiar case of verbal disputes in which the argument is not about the truth of certain ideas but about the meanings of words. How, he asks, can words be said to cause ideas when the same word can mean many things to many people?[33]

Fourth, Augustine holds that even agreement on the meaning of a set of symbols is no guarantee that meaning has been conveyed. Augustine uses the example that sometimes we fail to hear clearly and mistake one word for another. In such cases people can disagree about things even when the words about which they disagree have not been spoken.[34]

Augustine has another argument in this connection. "If we consider this more carefully, then perhaps you may find that there is nothing which is learned by means of signs. For when a sign is given me, if it finds me not knowing of what thing it is a sign, it can teach me nothing, but if it finds me knowing the thing of which it is the sign, what do I learn from the sign?"[35] Let us suppose, he writes, that I am reading a Latin version of the Biblical book of *Daniel* and in my reading I come across the word *sarabellae*. If I do not know the thing signified by *sarabellae*, then I cannot possibly know what the term means. If I have never encountered in my experience the *signifibilia* of the term, it will be just as useless to offer me synonyms either in Latin or in some other language. "For

it is the truest reasoning and most correctly said that when words are uttered we either know already what they signify or we do not know; if we know, then we remember rather than learn, but if we do not know, then we do not even remember, though perhaps we are prompted to ask."[36]

All this suggests for Augustine that what we take to be significant dialogues often turn out to be nothing more than insignificant monologues, because people are not really communicating their ideas. In the light of these difficulties how is teaching possible?

Like Plato before him, Augustine seems to be led to the strange conclusion that learning is impossible. However, instead of resolving that teaching is useless, he argues that teaching and learning are quite different from what they usually are thought to be. Knowledge of *a priori* truth cannot be passed from one person to another. It always arises within the soul. The student learns by consulting the truth present within his own mind. Communicating and teaching are possible only because the student already possesses truth. "Words possess only sufficient efficacy to remind us in order that we may seek things, but not to exhibit the things so that we may know them."[37] If the words spoken concur with the truth that the pupil finds within, he judges the statement to be true. On the other hand, should a teacher say that seven plus five are ten, the pupil—if he is sufficiently aware of the truth within—can judge the teacher to be in error. Augustine said, "Accordingly, even though I speak about true things, I still do not teach him who beholds the true things, for he is taught not through my words but by means of the things themselves which God reveals within the soul."[38] Thus, there is a sense in which the pupil sits in judgment over his teacher. The true teacher is Christ, who Himself is the truth and who in

the words of the fourth Gospel "lighteth every man that cometh into the world."[39]

Man does not learn truth about forms through teaching. As Adeodatus says in the conclusion to *De magistro,* man learns in the sense that words prompt him to remember the truth that is within his own soul. How this applies to the case of the *rationes aeternae* can be seen in Augustine's writing: "Concerning universals of which we can have knowledge, we do not listen to anyone speaking and making sounds outside ourselves. We listen to Truth which presides over our minds within us, though of course we may be bidden to listen by someone using words. Our real Teacher is he who is so listened to, who is said to dwell in the inner man, namely, Christ, that is, the unchangeable power and eternal wisdom of God."[40] While Augustine's language sounds mystical, his point is philosophical. Man knows the forms because God endows him with this knowledge and continually sustains his intellect in the knowing process.

But if man cannot come to know the eternal forms through experience, through Platonic reminiscence, or through teaching, how can we know them? Augustine's answer is divine illumination.

In his many references to the function of the divine light in making knowledge possible Augustine depends a great deal upon the analogy between physical and mental sight. In fact he often seems to use this analogy as an argument for the existence of an incorporeal light. "But we ought rather to believe, that the intellectual mind is so formed in its nature as to see these things, which by the disposition of the Creator are subjoined to things intelligible in a natural order, by a sort of incorporeal light of an unique kind; as the eye of the flesh sees things adjacent to itself in this bodily light, of which light it is made to be receptive, and adapted to it."[41] There is a

parallel between the eye's seeing corporeal objects and the mind's "seeing" incorporeal truth.[42] God is to the soul what the sun is to the eye. God is not only the truth in, by, and through whom all truths are true. He is not only the wisdom in, by, and through whom all wise men are made wise. He is also the light in, by, and through whom all intelligible things are illumined.[43]

> God, of course, belongs to the realm of intelligible things, and so do these mathematical symbols, though there is a great difference. Similarly the earth and light are visible, but the earth cannot be seen unless it is illumined. Anyone who knows the mathematical symbols admits that they are true without the shadow of a doubt. But he must also believe that they cannot be known unless they are illumined by something else corresponding to the sun. About this corporeal light notice three things. It exists. It shines. It illumines. So in knowing the hidden God you must observe three things. He exists. He is known. He causes other things to be known.[44]

Augustine's theory of illumination includes at least three major points: (1) God is light and illumines all men to different degrees; (2) There are intelligible truths, the *rationes aeternae*, which God illumines; and (3) The mind of man can know the divine truths only as God illumines him.

The importance of this doctrine to his entire theory of knowledge is indicated in an often-ignored passage in *Epistle* 120, where Augustine writes that the light makes us aware "of what we believe without knowing it, what we hold as objects of knowledge, what physical shape we recall, what one we imagine, what the sense-organ perceives, what the mind imagines in the likeness of a body, what is present to the intellect as certain yet totally unlike any physical object."[45] Thus, illumination plays a part in believing, knowing, remembering, imagining, sensing,

and, in fact, in every area of knowledge. He also uses his doctrine of the divine light to make the point that no soul is self-sufficient; no soul can be a light unto itself. Instead our minds must be illumined by participation in God's light. Whatever we do—thinking, speaking, or acting—we need the help of God. No other important aspect of Augustine's philosophy has proved as difficult to understand and to explain as this notion that God in some way illumines the mind of man.

chapter
seven : intellection, three interpretations of illumination

Differences about how Augustine's doctrine of illumination should be interpreted have engendered controversies on numerous side issues. The four major interpretations of Augustine's theory of illumination have been the Thomist, the Franciscan, the Formal, and the Ontologist. The first three positions will be studied in this chapter.

St. Thomas Aquinas interpreted Aristotle's vague remarks about the active intellect[1] as referring to something that is individual and particular in each man. Aquinas believed that this active intellect illumines the phantasm received by the passive intellect and abstracts the universal element involved from the phantasm. In *Summa Theologica* St. Thomas suggested that the light by which man's mind knows is the agent intellect.[2] He added that because God is the cause of the agent intellect, this gives the "light" a divine origin. Aquinas provided a further explanation of his position in *De Veritate* where he wrote:

> Therefore, man gains knowledge of things he does not know through two things: intellectual light and self-evident primary concepts. The latter have the same

relation to the intellectual light of the agent intellect as tools to the craftsman. Now, God in a most excellent way causes man's knowledge in both of these ways. For He adorned the soul itself with intellectual light and imprinted on it the concepts of the first principles, which are, as it were, the sciences in embryo, just as He impressed on other physical things the seminal principles for producing all their effects.[3]

Perhaps the best-known representative of this interpretation in the twentieth century has been Father Charles Boyer.[4] In his work *L'idée de vérité dans la philosophie de s. Augustin* he gives a concise statement of this approach.

God enlightens us by the very fact that our own intelligence enlightens us. Our intellect is, in fact, nothing else than the divine Light tempered to the infirmity of our nature. The truths we perceive are partial, limited, made clumsy by the multiplicity of the terms. Nevertheless, they are the expression, suited to our nature, of the total and simple truth, which is God. No one of our ideas in its positive content, expresses something which belongs to God, although under a form which the idea does not reveal. This is the sense in which God is our Light and the manner in which we see truths in God.[5]

An important aspect of the debate over this interpretation concerns Acquinas' interpretation of a passage in *De Trinitate*. The passage in Haddan's translation reads, "But we ought rather to believe, that the intellectual mind is so formed in its nature as to see these things, which by the disposition of the Creator are subjoined to things intelligible in a natural order, by a sort of incorporeal light of *an unique kind (sui generis).*"[6] Aquinas[7] insists that *sui generis* should be translated "of the same kind as it is," which would suggest that the light is of the same substance as mind. On the other hand, Gilson has contended that the phrase means simply "of a particular

kind."[8] In other words, in Aquinas' translation the text tends to support his claim that the divine light belongs in some sense to man's mind. This translation seems to have been shaped more by a predisposition to find a proof for Aquinas' identification of the divine light with the agent intellect than by a judicious consideration of the context. Gilson seems to be correct when he suggests that the phrase in question (*sui generis*) refers neither to God nor to the human intellect but serves instead to place in juxtaposition the corporeal nature of sight, on the one hand, and the spiritual nature of mind, on the other. The text teaches nothing more than that both man's mind and light are incorporeal; therefore, no support can be found for any identification of the divine light with the active intellect.

One problem with the Thomist interpretation is that it ignores the fact that Augustine's philosophical heritage was Platonism and not Aristotelianism—providing, of course, that we grant the reliability of St. Thomas' interpretation of Aristotle. Since the notion of abstraction belongs more to Aquinas than to Aristotle, however, the Thomistic interpretation of Augustine's view is anachronous. Also, a careful study of Augustine's philosophy should reveal that there is no room in his thought for any theory of abstraction. It is clear that for Augustine, as for Plato, there is no universal in the phantasm to be abstracted.

Almost without exception contemporary scholars agree that whatever virtue Aquinas' theory may have had as an independent position, it cannot draw support from Augustine.[9] One says that St. Thomas was aware that he was not being faithful to Augustine's original meaning. Miss Scheutzinger adds that whatever Aquinas' theory of the divine light is in its own right, it certainly is "not a misunderstanding of Saint Augustine—it is rather a masterpiece of philosophic diplomacy fitted into the conditions of Saint Thomas' age."[10] While this speaks well of

Acquinas' acumen, it seems to require an end to any more attempts to substantiate the agent intellect theory as a representation of the real meaning of Augustine's doctrine of illumination.

The Franciscan theory departs from the Thomist approach by ascribing the function of the agent intellect to God. The divine illumination is found chiefly in God's production, infusion, or impression of the divine forms upon the mind of man. These infused forms then become the first objects man knows or the norms by which he judges experience. Portalié in his famous article on Augustine in *Dictionnaire de Théologie Catholique*[11] describes this theory sympathetically: "In Scholastic language, the role of producing the impressed species which the Aristotelians attribute to the agent intellect is assigned to God in this system. . . . He imprints the representation of the eternal truths which is the cause of our knowledge. The ideas are not innate as in the angels but successively produced in the soul which knows them in itself."[12]

Portalié cites Bonaventure and Leibniz as earlier adherents of this interpretation, and he might also have included William of Auvergne and Roger Bacon. Those who presently interpret Augustine in this way are divided by the question of whether or not the forms are innate.[13]

Copleston and Gilson are among those who recently have criticized this theory. Copleston, for example, is bothered by the fact that in his understanding of the interpretation the human intellect need not play an active role in knowing.[14] If knowledge is the result of God's infusing ideas into man's mind, then the only part the mind plays is that of a passive receptor. However, if the infused ideas are regarded as present virtually or nonconsciously in the mind as predispositions to know or to recognize certain things, then for Augustine the mind is as active as it was for Kant.

Copleston offers another objection and appeals for sup-

port to the analogy Augustine frequently draws between the sun and divine illumination. The function of the sun, Copleston argues, is to make corporeal objects visible and not to create images or concepts in man's mind. Thus, he claims, for Augustine, God's light makes truth knowable but does not impress concepts. It might be possible to circumvent Copleston's point by arguing that he derives more from Augustine's analogy than Augustine himself did. It is easy to take a metaphor in literature and make it teach more than was intended.

Finally, both Copleston and Gilson have argued that Augustine's illumination theory was chiefly concerned with explaining the quality of certain ideas (*i.e.*, their certainty) and not their content. Thus, they hold, we do not see beauty itself. Instead, the idea of beauty illumines our minds so that we are able to judge beautiful objects. As it stands, though, this last point is not a criticism but only the assertion of an alternative interpretation of Augustine that still must be evaluated.

Although the Formal approach to Augustine's illumination theory has at times been coupled with a Thomistic notion of abstraction, its most characteristic element is its emphasis on the purely formal nature of God's illuminating activity. The function of illumination, according to this interpretation, is not to give the human mind some definite content of knowledge but simply to convey the quality of certainty and necessity to certain ideas. As Vernon J. Bourke writes, "St. Augustine's divine illumination doctrine is not so much a theory of the origin of concepts as of the manner in which the human mind is enabled to make some *judgments* with certitude. These judgments correspond with those which would be called first principles of logic, mathematics, morals and possibly metaphysics, in later scholasticism."[15] Others who have advanced this view in this century are Gilson, Copleston, Maurice DeWulf,[16] and Bern Kaelin.[17]

The main difference between the Franciscan interpretation and the Formal theory lies in their answers to the question of whether the divine illumination is concerned with the *origin* of our ideas or merely with the ground of their certitude. Was Augustine mainly trying to show that God is the efficient cause of our ideas, or was he trying to explain why certain ideas are necessary and immutable?

Gilson is convinced that the latter answer best explains Augustine's thought. Gilson disavows any role of the supernatural in human knowledge. For him our intellect always remains ours, not that of God or anyone else. Our thinking about truth is a natural process and is in complete accord with the natural (albeit God-ordained) course of reality. However, divine illumination is needed to make this possible. What Augustine's illumination theory reveals, Gilson contends, is that our judgments are true. It has nothing to do with the contents of the mind's ideas. As Gilson understands it, illumination concerns "not so much the power to conceive as the power to judge."[18] He believes that one of the strongest supports for this interpretation is its ability to do justice to both the Augustine texts that suggest the intellect is active and those that imply it is passive.

Perhaps too much has been made of the disjunction between content and quality, between the notion that illumination conveys some definite concepts and the theory that it simply makes necessary certain judgments. If there is no abstraction and no agent intellect in Augustine, then illumination must convey some content of knowledge. Copleston makes an interesting admission when he writes, "Whether Augustine explicitly says so or not, his view, as interpreted above, would at least demand abstraction in some form."[19] In other words, Copleston admits that even though Augustine never said anything about abstraction, an acceptance of Copleston's

interpretation requires that we readjust Augustine's thought to allow a doctrine that is contrary to the spirit of his philosophy. Therefore, if we admit that for Augustine concepts cannot be abstracted from phantasms received through the senses (primarily because there are no universals to be abstracted),[20] then the presence of the universal in the mind must be explained in some other way. The only remaining alternative that is consistent with the rest of Augustine's thought is that their presence in the mind results in some way from the activity of God.

One important function of illumination is the impression of formal certainty upon some judgments of the human mind. But it is wrong to go from this point and deny, as Gilson and Copleston do, that there is any material content conveyed by God's illumination of the soul. This not only conflicts with numerous texts, but it also leaves a huge gap in Augustine's theory of knowledge, implying that Augustine gives no explanation of how the soul acquires ideas of universals. This problem pushes Copleston to seek an abstraction that cannot be discovered in Augustine. Gilson wisely rejects this move, but he tries to avoid the problems raised in leaving such a lacuna in Augustine's thought by arguing that perhaps Augustine's interpreters are trying to "make him solve a problem which he did not expressly raise and which, perhaps, the basic tendencies of his doctrine excluded."[21] Gilson suggests that if we view things from Augustine's perspective and do not assume principles that Augustine himself rejected, we may find that there is no gap to be filled. "Actually, in Augustine there is no problem involving an *Umsetzung* (transformation) of the sensible thing into the intelligible. If he did not solve this problem, the reason was that he had no such problem to solve. If we insist that he solve it, then we do not fill a lacuna in his doctrine but change it into something else and in doing so take on ourselves the responsibility of foisting it on him."[22]

The major defect in Gilson's argument may be that it is too simple. His view does not provide an adequate basis for explaining all the major texts dealing with the subject. Many find it surprising that a thinker of Augustine's stature could have been blind to the problems that could arise if the question of how the soul forms it notions of universal ideas were to go unanswered. In many ways we are at the cornerstone of Augustine's entire theory of knowledge. Should we find that there is no cornerstone, then the entire superstructure might crumble. It does not seem, then, that the entire problem should be shunted away as if it did not exist. That there is no answer on Gilson's grounds need not bother us (unless we accept his presuppositions), for all one has to do is to abandon these grounds. If no answer is found on any grounds, however, Augustine and his theory of knowledge may have to be rejected.

Three interpretations of Augustine's illumination theory have been discussed. The most unsatisfactory of these appears to be the Thomist interpretation, and we can assume that this position has been refuted. The Formal interpretation (that of Gilson and Copleston) is correct in what it asserts (in the sense that illumination explains the certainty and necessity that attend many of our judgments) but wrong in what it denies. It fails to go far enough because of its refusal to allow any specific conceptual content to divine illumination. No serious objections could be found against the Franciscan theory, although, as in the case of the Formal interpretation, we may find that it does not say quite enough. The Ontologist interpretation remains to be examined.

chapter
eight : intellection,
the problem
of ontologism

IT is difficult to state the Ontologist interpretation
of Augustine's illumination theory in a concise yet clear
fashion. Advocates of this view hold that in some way
man can have a direct knowledge of the divine ideas,
that man "sees" the ideas that subsist in the mind of God.

Two factors make it difficult to get a clear and objective
picture of this theory. First of all, most Thomists[1] have
a vested interest in trying to refute Ontologism. Ontologism
seems to imply that if man can see the divine ideas in
this life, then he can also see God. If it is maintained
that the soul in some sense sees absolute truth, then it
follows that the soul sees God, since He is absolute truth.
The Thomist reserves this vision of God for either the
blessed in Heaven (the beatific vision) or for the few who
in this life attain a mystical experience of God. The
Thomist cannot deny that he would be embarrassed if
Ontologism should be found in such a father of the church
as St. Augustine. Many Christians, however, do not have
such theological qualms about a qualified Ontologism.

There is a second obstacle to the understanding of the
ontologist interpretation. All too often Malebranche, the
French philosopher of the seventeenth century, is con-

sidered to be the best representative of Ontologism. Malebranche did talk about illumination and did claim, citing Augustine as his authority, that "we see all things in God,"[2] but Malebranche's Ontologism is far removed from anything that might be found in Augustine. It should also be understood that criticisms of Malebranche are not necessarily valid when applied to Augustine.

Malebranche followed Descartes to the extent that he believed that all created reality is either extended substance (body) or thinking substance (mind). But according to Malebranche and contrary to Descartes, these two substances are so disparate that neither can have any causal effect on the other; there can be no interaction between mind and body. Perhaps the most important application of this doctrine can be found in Malebranche's view of man, particularly in his doctrine of human knowledge. Although man is a composite of body and soul, there can be no interaction between the two aspects of his existence. How, then, can man attain a knowledge of the sensible world, since this knowledge depends upon the sense organs' furnishing of information to the soul? This marks a major departure from Augustine, for while he regarded man as a being composed of two substances, body and soul, he believed that the two components could influence each other. For Augustine this was especially true in the case of sensation, although, of course, the influence between body and soul always was initiated in the activity of the soul. Man receives information about the physical world through the senses of his body. Malebranche could not maintain this, and he had to find another way to account for man's knowledge of sensible world. When Malebranche said that we see all things in God, he truly meant all things. Though his view does not preclude sensations in the body, it does rule out any causal connection between bodily sensations and the psychic events that follow them. Malebranche believed that God causes even

the images or ideas that we have of sensible things, and he made this clear when he wrote, "We believe also that one knows changing and corruptible things in God, although St. Augustine talks only of immutable and incorruptible things."[3] Thus, in Malebranche's Ontologism man sees not only the eternal truths but also ideas of the particular things in God's creation. There are difficulties in interpreting some of the things that Malebranche said, but these need not concern us here. The important point is that the consideration of Malebranche as a representative of the ontologist interpretation of Augustine does an injustice to Augustine's thought and causes great confusion. For example, at times the criticisms raised against Ontologism apply only to Malebranche and are not relevant to the kind of Ontologism found in Augustine.

Any adequate account of Augustine's theory of knowledge in general and of his doctrine of illumination in particular must deal satisfactorily with three paradoxes in his thought. First, Augustine seems to teach that the intellect is both active and passive. Second, he teaches that the forms are distinct from and not distinct from the human mind. Third, he writes that man's mind is and is not the light that makes knowledge possible.

In many writings Augustine suggests that man's intellect is passive. In *De ordine* he speaks of the law of God being transcribed upon the soul of man.[4] In *De Trinitate* he affirms that the rules by which men make moral judgments are impressed upon man's heart as a seal is impressed upon wax.[5] Augustine's point with reference to the forms is analogous to an empiricist's analysis of sense perception. Man does not create the sensible objects he experiences, for they appear to him in certain regular ways. Regardless of how man might want the world to be, certain appearances seem to force themselves upon his mind; they are given. According to Augustine man does not create the eternal forms. They are

a given and he must receive them as they are impressed upon his mind. There are passages that suggest that the mind is completely passive in its reception of the divine ideas.

But man does not simply receive a knowledge of the forms. As noted before, *scientia* is possible because man can bring eternal standards of judgment to bear upon sense images. This clearly implies that the mind plays an active role in knowledge.

With respect to the second paradox, Augustine teaches first that the forms are and must be distinct from the human intellect. In *De Trinitate* he speaks of the forms as "above the eye of the mind."[6] One of the important arguments of *De libero arbitrio* is that truth is superior to the human mind.[7] Again in *De Trinitate* he explains that unless the forms "were above the human mind, [they] would certainly not be unchangeable."[8] If the *rationes aeternae* are not distinct from man's mind, they will suffer from the same mutability and finiteness that characterize human reason. However, the same passage adds that "unless something of our own [mind] were subjoined to them [the forms], we should not be able to employ them as our measures by which to judge of corporeal things."

Many passages in Augustine suggest that the forms are part of man's rational nature. In his *Confessions* Augustine writes, "The memory contains also the reasons and innumerable laws of numbers and dimensions, none of which has any sense of the body impressed."[9] In *De immortalitate animae* he teaches that "when we reason with ourselves or some other person asks us skillful questions, we discover (*invenire*) truth in our minds."[10] Later in the same work he comments, "Those things that are comprehended by the intellect, however, are comprehended as existing nowhere else but in the comprehending mind itself, and, at the same time, as not contained in space."[11] He asks how we could see that some things are good and better

than other things "unless a conception *(notio)* of the good itself had been impressed upon us, such that according to it we might both approve some things as good and prefer one good to another."[12]

One of the most important passages in this connection is found in the eighth book of *De civitate Dei:* "For there is no corporeal beauty, whether in the condition of a body, as figure, or in its movement, as in music, of which it is not the mind that judges. But this could never have been, had there not existed *in the mind itself* a superior form of these things, without bulk, without noise of voice, without space and time."[13]

This passage states something more than that the forms must be related to the mind. It states specifically that the mind could not judge unless these ideas actually existed in the mind. But, he continues, the presence of these forms in the mind does not make the mind immutable. "But even in respect of these things, had the mind not been mutable, it would not have been possible for one to judge better than another with regard to sensible forms. He who is clever, judges better than he who is slow, he who is skilled than he who is unskilled, he who is practiced than he who is unpracticed; and the same person judges better after he has gained experience than he did before."[14]

The differences that one finds in human minds, however, suggest that man's reason continues mutable, even though the forms may exist within it.

> Whence able men, who have thought deeply on these things, have gathered that the first form is not to be found in those things whose form is changeable. Since, therefore, they saw that body and mind might be more or less beautiful in form, and that, if they wanted [*i.e.,* lacked] form, they [body and mind] could have no existence, they saw that there is some existence in which is the first form, unchangeable, and therefore not ad-

mitting of degrees of comparison, and in that they most rightly believed was the first principle of things which was not made, and by which all things were made.[15]

Unless particular things possessed some form (in the sense that they are patterned after an eternal archetype), they would not exist, because the eternal forms are *formae principales*, a necessary condition of all creation.[16] Everything that exists has the ground of its intelligibility in a corresponding form. However, because the forms of particular things vary (for example, "body and mind might be more or less beautiful in form"),[17] this suggests to Augustine that there is some unchanging existence that is the primary form. This first form is not only immutable, but it also does not admit of degrees of comparison. It is, in fact, "the first principle of things which was not made, and by which all things were made." This first form is either God or the divine idea that subsists in the mind of God.[18]

Thus, this passage in *De civitate Dei* teaches that there are three modes of existence in which the forms may be found. First is the form that appears to be the eternal archetype subsisting in the mind of God. There is secondly the form that particular things possess by virtue of their creation after the eternal pattern. Because particular things imitate the divine pattern to varying degrees, this form is mutable. Finally, there is the sense in which forms exist in the mind of man. Man's possession of the forms makes *scientia* possible.

Turning finally to the third paradox, Augustine asserts that the light that makes knowledge possible does not designate man's reason. "The light of minds is above minds and surpasses all minds."[19] However, in *Contra Faustum Manichaeum*[20] Augustine teaches that there is a sense in which the changeable and finite mind of man *is* a light. This last passage merits special study, because

it may hold the key that will make possible a resolution of the three paradoxes.

Augustine teaches that the mind of man is a created intelligible light.

> And, again, the act of forming a conception of Alexandria, which I have never seen, is very different from thinking of Carthage, which I know. But this difference is insignificant as compared with that between my thinking of material things which I know from seeing them, and my understanding justice, chastity, faith, truth, love, goodness, and things of this nature. Can you describe this intellectual light, which gives us a clear perception of the distinction between itself and other things, as well as of the distinction between those things themselves? And yet even this is not the sense in which it can be said that God is light, for *this light is created*, whereas God is the Creator; *the light is made* and He is the Maker; *the light is changeable*. For the intellect changes from dislike to desire, from ignorance to knowledge, from forgetfulness to recollection; whereas God remains the same in will, in truth and in eternity.[21]

This passage resolves the paradox about whether or not the mind of man is the light that makes knowledge possible by suggesting that there are actually two lights that make knowledge possible—the uncreated light of God and the created, mutable light, which is man's intellect. Just as the moon derives the light it reflects from the sun, so the rational mind of man derives a created ability to know from its origin, God. The knowledge possessed by man can be regarded as a reflection of the truth originating in the mind of God. But man's mind and the knowledge he has are in one important respect perfectly natural (as opposed to supernatural), since the knowledge is derived from rational capacities that are an inherent part of man's nature.

A synthesis of all the passages that have a bearing on the soul's relation to the forms leads to the view that

these ideas in the mind (or memory) are (1) *a priori*, (2) virtual, (3) preconditions of *scientia*.

They are, to use Kant's term, *a priori* because they cannot be derived from experience. They are virtual because they are said to be in the mind or memory, even when they are not objects of thought. For example, "there can be something in the mind, which the mind itself does not perceive to be in it."[22] Augustine is thinking here of the art of music, but his remarks also apply to the principles of other sciences, such as geometry. Finally, the ideas are preconditions of *scientia* because knowledge becomes possible only when these universals are applied to the images from sensation.

One reason that Augustine can speak of man's mind as a created light is because he believes that the forms are in some sense in the mind of man. In *De libero arbitrio* Augustine writes that the laws by which we judge beauty are in the mind. "You will return to your mind within, and know that you could neither approve nor disapprove things of sense unless you had within you, as it were, laws of beauty by which you judge all beautiful things which you perceive in the world."[23] This is also true in the case of goodness itself. We would be unable to make value judgments "unless a conception *(notio)* of the good itself had been impressed upon us."[24]

This is taken to mean that God has endowed man with a structure of rationality patterned after the divine ideas in His own mind. Man can know truth because God has made man like Himself. If this claim is true, it helps to explain how man can know not only the eternal forms but also the creation that is patterned after these forms. Man can know the corporeal world only because he first knows and understands the intelligible world. Man possesses as an inherent part of his nature forms of thought by which he knows and judges sensible things.

This interpretation of Augustine finds an element of

truth in the Franciscan theory. However, this interpretation parts with Portalié, who denied that the ideas are innate[25] and concurs with the view of Richard Ackworth, who writes:

> St. Augustine's view seems to have been that these *a priori* standards or *notiones impressae* are originally virtual or nonconscious and of the nature of predispositions to recognize, for instance, imperfect goodness in the light of perfect goodness; we come consciously to know them only by reflecting on the judgments made in their light. But the *notio* of goodness is not abstracted from the objects judged to be good, for it had to be virtually present *a priori* for us to be able to recognize them as good at all.[26]

It may already be possible to see how the three paradoxes can be resolved. The paradox about whether the mind is or is not a light that makes knowledge possible is resolved when one sees that there are really two lights— the created, intelligible light that is man's mind and the uncreated, intelligible light that is God. The paradox concerning the relation of the forms to man's mind is partially resolved by the view that the forms exist first (temporally, logically, and ontologically) in the mind of God and exist in a derived form in the rational structure of man's mind. The paradox about whether man's mind is active or passive may be the easiest to resolve. For the most part man's mind is passive with regard to universals (although man can bring his rational powers into play in order to sharpen his understanding of these ideas) and active with regard to knowledge (*scientia*) of corporeal things known through the senses. The mind is active in *scientia* because sensible things must be judged according to the standards of the universals.

While the mind of man is necessary if he is to know truth, it is not sufficient. According to Augustine, the created light of man's intellect needs a light from with-

out.[27] Even the created intelligible light would be unable to account for man's knowledge without the constant, immanent, and active presence of God.

> But different is the light itself by which the soul is illumined that it may see everything it apprehends with truth through the intellect, either in itself or *in this light*; for the light is God Himself, and the soul a creature made rational and intellectual in His image and whenever it tries to look upon that light it struggles feebly and fails. Nevertheless from this light comes all that it apprehends by the intellect as well as it can.[28]

Contrary to Portalié, God is not some kind of external agent intellect. Man's possession of the forms of thought is something natural, inasmuch as he possesses them from the time his life begins. They are part of the rational structure of his mind and are his by virtue of his creation in the image of God. However, we must not think of the forms as having been given to man once-and-for-all. Augustine is clear in stating that the soul never ceases to be dependent upon God for its knowledge. "God, having so made man, has not left him deistically, to himself, but continually reflects into his soul the contents of His own eternal and immutable mind—which are precisely those eternal and immutable truths which constitute the intelligible world. The soul is therefore in unbroken communion with God, and in the body of intelligible truths reflected into it from God, sees God."[29]

Thus, knowledge is possible because God has created man after his own image as a rational soul and because God continually sustains and aids the soul in its quest for knowledge. The argument thus far has been constructed from points in both the Franciscan and Formal interpretations of Augustine's illumination theory and may also gain from Ontologism.

The Augustinian texts that appear to teach Ontologism are well known to the critics of this view. Before any of

the passages are examined here, the various means that the critics will use to avoid the ontologist interpretation should be noted. This will allow a more careful evaluation of each text. Etienne Gilson will be used as a representative critic of Ontologism. He not only is an acknowledged authority on Augustine, but he also does not shirk his responsibility of meeting the challenges posed by the ontologist texts. Gilson deals with these passages in three basic ways.

First, he appeals to the fact in many of them Augustine speaks in metaphors.[30] We should beware of basing a doctrine—especially one as debatable as Ontologism—on metaphorical statements. It is not easy to know which of the many points suggested by an analogy are considered by the author to be relevant. For example, some writers, commenting upon the analogy between the divine light and the light of the sun, have said that the function of the corporeal light is to illumine other objects and not to draw attention to itself.[31] Likewise, they argue, the function of the divine light must be to illumine its objects, the eternal truths, and not to make possible a knowledge of the source of the light. Thus, Augustine's actual metaphor of light is appealed to in supporting a criticism of Ontologism. The argument is raised here not for criticism but as an example of the diverse uses to which analogy can be put.

Gilson's second approach to the ontologist texts holds that sometimes when Augustine talks about a direct vision of truth or the divine ideas, he is referring to a mystical experience and not to our natural knowledge.[32] This move, however, provides a readymade trashbasket into which a careless critic of Ontologism might throw any problem text. The appeal to mysticism is not wrong, however, and one can hardly deny the mystical element in Augusine's experiences and writings, but the argument must be used with care and discrimination.[33]

Gilson's third move suggests that the passages which cannot be handled in the first two ways imply at the most that the forms which man is said to see have only a regulative function.[34] Since they convey no content, they cannot give man a vision of God.

The ontologist texts can be conveniently divided into four groups.

Three passages—*Confession* VII, 17; *De Trinitate* VIII, 3; and *De civitate Dei* XI, 2—are relevant to the question of whether Gilson's appeal to mysticism is valid.

In the passage from the *Confessions* Augustine traces the process by which he discovered unchanging and eternal truth above his mutable mind. First, he passed from the outer to the inner world; *i.e.*, he passed from the realm of bodies to the world of the soul, which perceives by means of the bodily senses. Then he passed from the lower to the higher capacities of the soul; *i.e.*, he moved from the lower reason, which judges sensible things, to the higher reason, which knows unchanging truth.

> That so it might find out that light by which it was besprinkled, when, without all doubting, it cried out, that the unchangeable was to be preferred before the changeable; whence also it knew no sure ground for preferring it to the changeable. And thus, with the flash of a trembling glance, it arrived at that which is. And then I saw thy invisible things understood by the things that are made. But I was not able to fix my gaze thereon; and my infirmity being beaten back, I was thrown again on my accustomed habits, carrying along with me naught but a loving memory thereof, and an appetite for what I had, as it were, smelt the odor of, but was not yet able to eat.[35]

Augustine's meaning is obscured somewhat by the translation. He is really claiming to have "arrived at That Which Is," or God.[36] Gilson's answer to the text is that this last step in which the soul sees God is mysticism.[37]

Gilson's interpretation is extremely plausible, but another interpretation should be considered. The passage in question may be advancing either mysticism or Platonism. *Confessions* VII, 17 might be sketching an assent to God similar to that presented in *De libero arbitrio.*[38] In the latter work Augustine explains how man can ascend the scale of being from the level of bare existence (for example, stones exist but do not possess life), to the level of sensation (shared with the brutes), to the level of reason, and finally to that eternal and unchangeable reality which is above reason—God. This passage in the *Confessions* may be an outline of his search for truth and his discovery of the author of truth. First he passed from the world of bodies, which is mutable in space and time, to the world of the soul, which is mutable in time. Then he passed from the lower reason, which judges sensation, to the superior reason, which knows unchangeable truth. But as was the case in *De libero arbitrio,* there is a reality that is yet higher than reason, and occasionally Augustine has even seen God, who is the author of truth.

Either interpretation of this passage in the *Confessions* is plausible. What is needed to tip the scales is another passage sufficiently similar to the text in question to invite comparison.

In *De Trinitate*[39] Augustine refers to the many types of judgments that we make about the goodness of things. We judge that fertile earth, well-managed households, animate bodies, air, agreeable food, health, friends, and many other things are good. "And why add yet more and more? This thing is good and that good, but take away this and that, and regard good itself if thou canst; so wilt thou see God, not good by a good that is other than Himself, but the good of all good."[40] Again, the translation would have been clearer had it capitalized the important phrase "Good itself," for what is at stake is the mind passing above particular things that are said

to be good and arriving at God who is goodness itself. It seems obvious that there is no question of mysticism in this passage.

> Wherefore there would be no changeable goods, unless there were the unchangeable Good. Whenever then thou art told of this good thing and that good thing, which things can also in other respects be called not good, if thou canst put aside those things which are good by the participation of the Good, and discern that Good itself by the participation of which they are good. . . . if, then, I say thou canst remove these things, and canst discern the Good in itself, then thou wilt have discerned God.[41]

In this text the soul rises above particular things, which are said to be good, to goodness itself, which is God. There is no hint of mysticism in the ascent. In the other text the soul rises above particular and changeable truths to truth itself, which is God. Since the sight of goodness itself does not involve mysticism, why must we conclude otherwise in the case of truth?

Another similar text is *De civitate Dei* XI, 2. "It is a great and very rare thing for a man, after he has contemplated the whole creation, corporeal and incorporeal, and has discerned its mutability, to pass beyond it, and, by the continued soaring of his mind, to attain to the unchangeable substance of God, and, in that height of contemplation, to learn from God Himself that none but He has made all that is not of the divine essence."[42]

Possibly what Augustine describes in this passage is mysticism, but it would be a kind of mysticism far removed from the usual meaning. William James regarded ineffability as one of four characteristics of a mystical experience. As James said, "No adequate report of its contents can be given in words. . . . No one can make clear to another who has never had a certain feeling, in what the quality or worth of it consists."[43] There is no

need to take James' word on this matter. Experiences that are commonly taken to be mystical do evidence this trait of ineffability. The agent finds himself incapable of describing just what it was that he experienced. But there is a cognitive element to the contemplation described in the passage from Augustine. Augustine *"learns* from God Himself" that God created all that is. If a true mystical experience is ineffable, then what Augustine describes in this passage is not mysticism.

Another point is relevant here. Critics of Ontologism often talk as if contemplation and mysticism are to be equated.[44] This identification seems doubtful, because Augustine teaches that "something divine and unchangeable is learned" in contemplation."[45] A contemplation that conveys cognitive meaning can hardly be equated with an ineffable experience. Furthermore, this identification ignores Augustine's remarks to the effect that *sapientia* makes use of the method of contemplation. Since *sapientia* includes the knowledge of unchangeable truth such as is found in mathematics and geometry, it again becomes difficult to see how this concerns mysticism.

The passages *Confessions* XII, 25 and *De Trinitate* IX, 7, 12 have in common a statement that we see truth in God. The text from *De Trinitate* reads, "We behold, then, by the sight of the mind, in that eternal truth from which all things temporal are made."[46] The passage from the *Confessions* is quite similar: "If we both see that that which thou sayest is true, and if we both see that what I say is true, where, I ask, do we see it? Certainly not I in thee, nor thou in me, but both in the unchangeable truth itself, which is above our minds."[47] Johannes Hessen, an advocate of Ontologism, suggests that when Augustine talks about a vision in truth,[48] he should be understood to mean a vision of truth, or a vision of God. Gilson turns this to his own advantage with the following argument. First, he compares the phrase "seeing in truth" with

"seeing in light." He then argues that when the soul no longer merely sees in the light but actually sees the light itself that this is mysticism.[49] Similarly, it must be concluded that if the soul sees truth itself, this too must be the result of a mystical experience. Gilson's analogy seems weak, however, because it ignores the point that while light illumines other objects, it also reveals something of its own nature. Even while the soul is seeing in the light (or in the truth, as the case may be), it may quite possibly see something of the light.

Gilson has a stronger argument, however. He admits that Augustine teaches that we see truth *in* God, but he refuses to allow that this means we have a vision *of* God. Gilson says this view would imply that even the most wicked men (who share the common lot of all mankind in being able to see truth *in* God) would have a mystical experience when they saw truth.[50] This is a difficult conclusion to accept. But does Ontologism imply this absurd notion?

It seems that a true mystical experience must have at least one characteristic. Regardless of how ecstatic the experience, the agent must at least be conscious that he is experiencing God. A mystical experience is surely more than this, but it cannot be less.

Because of their moral condition many men are incapable of being aware of God. Just as sin hinders man from seeing God in the creation,[51] so also sin keeps many from seeing God in the eternal truths. Plato's allegory of the cave provides a helpful illustration. Plato remarks that it is only with great effort that men ascend the cave. It is difficult to draw men away from the things of sense so that they may see the forms. Even after the forms are seen, it is even more demanding to ascend the rest of the way in order to view the sun, the form of the good. Had Augustine adopted this position with no modifications, it might support the claims of those who wish these

texts to teach mysticism. But Augustine did not separate the forms from God, as Plato did. They subsist in the mind of God so that he who perceives unchanging truth—whether he is aware of it or not—is in contact with the divine. Were men's minds not affected by sin, they would clearly see the eternal power and godhead of God in the visible creation, and they would recognize that in knowing truth they also know God. Even after a man's spiritual eyes have been opened so that he is able to see the evidence of God's existence in the creation, however, the awareness of God that he has does not produce a mystical experience. Similarly, when a man becomes aware that he knows something of God's nature through knowing truth, he is not necessarily a candidate for a mystical state. We conclude, therefore, that if a vision in truth is equivalent to a vision of truth (God), it does not imply the absurd consequences attributed to it by Gilson.

The texts *De Trinitate* XII, 14, 23 and XIV, 15, 21 are brought together because Gilson approaches them in the same way. The first passage reads: "And to attain to these [the forms] with the eye of the mind is the lot of few; and when they are attained as much as they can be, he himself who attains to them does not abide in them, but is as it were repelled by the rebounding of the eye itself of the mind.[52]

Augustine definitely states that we see the forms with the eye of the mind. The context of the second passage speaks of the rules by which men make moral judgments. He asks, "And where do they see these rules?" He will not allow that they are seen in man's own moral nature, for the rules are unchangeable and man's nature is mutable.

> Where indeed are these rules written, wherein even the unrighteous recognizes what is righteous, wherein he discerns that he ought to have what he himself has not? Where, then, are they written, unless in the book of that Light which is called Truth? Whence every

righteous law is copied and transferred (not by migrating to it, but by being as it were impressed upon it) to the heart of the man that worketh righteousness; as the impression from a ring passes into the wax, yet does not leave the ring.[53]

Both texts seem to bring man's mind into the kind of direct contact with the eternal forms that implies Ontologism. Gilson claims that regardless of what the passages seem to say, they do not imply Ontologism, because the action of the divine ideas is essentially regulative and has no content.[54] Even if we grant that the soul comes into direct contact with the divine ideas, this does not produce a knowledge of God, because the ideas themselves are void of any conceptual content. "For the divine idea is not knowledge which passes ready-made from God into the mind of man; it is a law which binds him—*lex incommutabilis*—which constrains him by its own necessity and in doing so bestows this necessity on him."[55] Gilson's case is strengthened, because several texts speak of the ideas as rules.[56] However, it appears that Gilson's argument will not cover at least one place in which Augustine draws a clear distinction between ideas and laws (rules). In *De libero arbitrio* Augustine distinguishes the idea of number from the laws of numbers.[57] Gilson is aware of this, but he persists in his attempt to show that the notions that God impresses on man's mind cannot be concepts but are instead rules.[58] The dispute over the so-called ontologist texts is not simply the result of difficulties in the passages themselves; rather, it is due largely to prior commitments to assumptions about what Augustine could and could not have believed.

The passages *De Trinitate* IX, 6, 9,; IX, 6, 11; and XII, 15, 24 all teach that the mind sees truth or sees the forms. The first states that "we gaze upon indestructible truth;"[59] the second teaches that we grasp the forms by simple intelligence;[60] and the last claims "that the intellectual mind

is so formed in its nature as to see those things, which by the disposition of the Creator are subjoined to things intelligible in a natural order, by a sort of incorporeal light of an unique kind."[61]

Gilson admits that there is nothing mystical in these passages. His only recourse is to urge that the texts should be interpreted by the rest of what Augustine wrote and that they should not become a basis on which the rest of Augustine's theory of knowledge is interpreted.[62] However, it is not merely two or three isolated texts that we must overlook. Because of the inadequate treatment Gilson gives many of the other ontologist texts, an acceptance of his repudiation of Ontologism seems to require that we also ignore them as well. As Augustine made clear, presuppositions are important. If one approaches Augustine's theory of knowledge with the assumption that Ontologism cannot be present because it is inconsistent with the Scriptures, then he will work hard to find some other meaning for the ontologist texts. On the other hand, if one comes to Augustine presupposing that Ontologism need not be avoided by a Christian philosopher, then he will find that many more passages in Augustine's writings can be taken at face value.

There is one more objection to Ontologism. Gilson argues that if it is possible for us to see things in God's ideas, then we could know these things without having to see them through the senses.[63] That is, because all corporeal things are particular copies of His ideas, God knows all things a priori. Augustine, however, reserved an important place for sense perception—something he would not have done if the ontologist interpretation were correct. Gilson concludes that if it is impossible to see God in a literal sense, it is just as impossible to see ideas that subsist in the mind of God. This argument is fallacious for two reasons. First, it applies only to the

kind of Ontologism advanced by Malebranche. The second point is related to the first. Illumination for Augustine reveals only universals and not particulars. Thus, Gilson's objection appears to be irrelevant.

The Ontologism that Augustine teaches is a modified Ontologism. The vision of God is qualitatively and quantitatively different from the beatific vision, but it is nonetheless a vision of God. "And hence, in so far as we know God, we are like Him, but not like to the point of equality, since we do not know Him to the extent of his own being."[64] While man can have some knowledge of God's nature in this life, it is limited. At best, in the words of St. Paul, "we see through a glass darkly."[65]

> The more ardently we love God, the more certainly and the more calmly do we see Him, because we behold in God the unchangeable form of righteousness, according to which we judge that man ought to live. Therefore, faith avails to the knowledge and to the love of God, not as though of one altogether unknown, or altogether not loved; but so that thereby He may be known more clearly, and loved more steadfastly.[66]

Gilson makes much of the difficulties that Augustine faced in identifying the respective roles that God and man play in knowledge. "Truth is too good for man. As soon as there is truth, there is God. How then can truth become ours? As long as it is God's truth, it is unchangeable and necessary, i.e., truth itself. As soon as it is created in us, it must be changeable, temporal and contingent. like the intellect which receives it. In this case, is it still the truth?"[67]

Gilson's point that truth is too good for man rings false when one considers all that Augustine taught. Truth is not difficult to find—just look within. It is not too good for man—just look within. Gilson confuses the distinction between immutable truth and the reception

of truth. That truth is grasped incompletely or inadequately does not affect truth itself. Gilson continues, "Since we have assumed that God gave us, not a Thomistic intellect which can produce truth, but a mind which is limited to receiving it, how can the divine light be brought to our minds and still remain divine?"[68]

Perhaps these words lay bare Gilson's difficulty. As long as one continues to think that a Thomistic intellect can produce truth by abstracting it in some way from sensation, he will be looking at Augustine's position from the outside. Augustine's point is that truth cannot be derived from sensation; it can only be imposed upon sensation by a mind that is aware of eternal truth. It is incorrect to speak of a Thomistic intellect that can produce truth and an Augustinian mind that can only receive it. For Augustine there are three levels of truth. There is truth itself (God); there are the eternal truths (the forms) that subsist in His mind; and there are true things that are mutable and can pass away. Augustine believes that God has endowed man with the ability to make true judgments, and though this truth may suffer necessarily from the same limitations as the human mind, it is still truth. Gilson ignores the fact that just as there are degrees of goodness in God's creation, so there are degrees of truth. True things partake of more or less truth, depending upon their participation in the absolute truth, which is God. Perhaps this point can be clarified by distinguishing among ideas, perceptions, and conceptions.[69] The ideas are the *rationes aeternae*, which remain unchangeable even when they are reflected into the mutable minds of men. "Perception" refers to the apprehension by men of the divine ideas. Because men's souls differ and even the same soul at different times may be found in different states of ability and awareness, these perceptions will be anything but immutable. The same can be said for con-

ceptions, which are knowledge built upon the bases of perception. Because man's mind plays a role in perceptions and conceptions, there will be varying results.

> If the condition of all knowledge, then, is revelation, and therefore all knowledge is in its source divine; yet it is equally true that the qualification of all knowledge is rooted in the human nature that knows, and in the specific state of the human being whose particular knowledge it is. It is in this fact that the varying degrees of purity in which knowledge is acquired by some men find their explanation.[70]

This does not eliminate the problem for Augustine, but it should suggest that the problem Augustine leaves is no greater than that faced by any theory of knowledge, ancient or modern. Gilson implies that Augustine's difficulty of relating the divine and human roles in knowledge is one that only Augustine faces. Augustine is using different terminology to refer to the difficulty of relating the universal and particular, reason and experience, the certain and probable, knowledge and belief. Augustine's answer—however adequate it may be—is more modern than many Thomists give him credit for. There is more than a hint in his works that Augustine was struggling to find a theory of knowledge that would combine the benefits of realism and conceptualism. Universals exist independently of particulars (in the mind of God), but they also exist in a secondary sense in the mind of man. Knowledge of the world is possible because God has patterned the world after the divine ideas. Man can know the world because God has given man an awareness of the eternal forms by which he can judge sensations and form *scientia*. Some Thomists have suggested that "skepticism in philosophy was the inevitable result of this concept of knowledge."[71] They can make this claim only because they have failed to drop all their Thomistic assumptions when approach-

ing Augustine, and they have thus been hindered in their attempt to enter completely into the spirit of his thought. Were Augustine able to answer in his defense, he might reply that skepticism in philosophy may be the inevitable result of abandoning this conception of knowledge.

bibliographical note

THE complete works of St. Augustine are found in Tomes XXXII to XLVII of *Patrologiae cursus completus, Patrum Latinorum*, edited by the Benedictines of the Congregation of St. Maur, J. P. Migne, editor. This work, published in 1861, is gradually being superseded by *Corpus Scriptorum ecclesiasticorium latinorum*, which, when completed, will contain the critical texts of all Augustine's writings. The Nicene and Post-Nicene Fathers, First Series, ed. Philip Schaff (Grand Rapids, Mich.: Eerdmans, 1956) contains *The Works of St. Augustine* in eight volumes. However, the translations are over eighty years old and the series omits many of Augustine's early philosophical writings. In 1947 the Catholic University of America Press began to publish the series Fathers of the Church. Thus far, twenty volumes of Augustine's writings have appeared including most of the major philosophical writings. Nine volumes of Augustine's writings have also appeared in the Ancient Christian Writers series, published by the Newman Press.

An excellent bibliography of books and articles published prior to 1960 appears in Etienne Gilson's *The Christian Philosophy of Saint Augustine* (New York: Random House, 1960). Important books that have appeared since 1960 include Vernon J. Bourke, *Augustine's View of Reality* (Villanova, Pa.: Villanova Press, 1964); John F.

Callahan, *Augustine and the Greek Philosophers* (Villanova, Pa.: Villanova Press, 1967); G. L. Keyes, *Christian Faith and the Interpretation of History* (Lincoln: University of Nebraska Press, 1966); John A. Mourant, *Introduction to the Philosophy of Saint Augustine* (University Park, Pa.: Pennsylvania State University Press, 1964); and A. D. R. Polman, *The Word of God According to St. Augustine* (Grand Rapids, Mich.: Eerdmans, 1961).

Gilson's bibliography omits a number of helpful studies including A. H. Armstrong, *The Architecture of the Intelligible Universe in the Philosophy of Plotinus* (Cambridge, Eng.: Cambridge University Press, 1940) A. H. Armstrong, *An Introduction to Ancient Philosophy* (London: Methuen and Co., 1947); Roy A. Battenhouse, ed., *A Companion to the Study of St. Augustine* (New York: Oxford University Press, 1955); John Burnaby, *Amor Dei* (London: Hodder and Stoughton, 1947); Mary T. Clarke, *Augustine, Philosopher of Freedom* (New York: Nesclée, 1958); C. N. Cochrane, *Christianity and Classical Culture* (London: Oxford, 1957); Sister Mary Patricia Garvey, *Saint Augustine, Christian or Neo-Platonist?* (Milwaukee: Marquette University Press, 1939); Richard Kroner, *Speculation and Revelation in the Age of Christian Philosophy* (Philadelphia: Westminster Press, 1959); and Harry Austryn Wolfson, *The Philosophy of the Church Fathers*, I (Cambridge, Mass.: Harvard University Press, 1956).

notes

Chapter One

¹ Frederick Copleston, *A History of Philosophy,* II: *Augustine to Scotus* (Westminster, Md.: The Newman Press, 1962), 49.

² Etienne Gilson, *The Christian Philosophy of Saint Augustine* (New York: Random House, 1960), 245.

³ "Introduction," *Basic Writings of Saint Augustine* (New York: Random House, 1948), I, x. Henceforth, this entire volume will be designated as *BWOA.*

⁴ Plato *Phaedrus* 275.

⁵ Those written to Nebridius about A.D. 389.

⁶ *De Trinitate* (finished in A.D. 416) and *De Genesi ad Litteram* (completed in A.D. 415).

⁷ Plotinus actually held that "Being" both descends from and ascends to The One. Since my purpose is only to examine the similarities between the Plotinian and Augustinian doctrines, only the first point is noted.

⁸ Plato *The Republic,* chap. 7.

⁹ See *De libero arbitrio* II, 3, 7 to II, 15, 39 and *Confessions* VII, 17. However, Augustine does not believe that man must necessarily begin with sensation. He also holds that it is possible to know and to prove God's existence apart from sensation.

¹⁰ *Confessions* XI, 4-5.

¹¹ *Ibid.* I, 4, trans. J. G. Pilkington in *The Nicene and Post-Nicene Fathers,* First Series, ed. Philip Schaff (Grand Rapids, Mich.: Eerdmans, 1956), III. Henceforth, this is to be designated as NPNF.

¹² Augustine's most complete account of the levels of reality is found in *De Gen. ad Litt.,* bk. I.

¹³ *Ibid.*

¹⁴ *De diversis quaestionibus* 46, 1-2.

¹⁵ Philo suggested that God created the world of Ideas to serve as a model for the visible world (*De opificio* IV, 16). However, one can also find in Philo the apparently contradictory notion that the world of Ideas is to be equated with the mind of God (*De opificio* VI, 24).

¹⁶ Plotinus understood the Platonic Ideas as thoughts of God and located them in *nous,* the first hypostasis emanating from The One.

¹⁷ One need not assume at this point that Augustine was consciously dependent on either Philo or Plotinus. He merely found himself in a similar position to that which Philo had occupied before him, *i.e.,* Augustine was forced to relate the eternal forms to the infinite God of the

Hebraic-Christian tradition. Given Augustine's understanding of the nature of God, it is difficult to see how he could have taken any other step.

[18] *De Trin.* XII, 15, 24-25; XIII, 1, 1-2; XIV, 1, 3; XIV, 6, 11.

[19] *Ibid.* XII, 3, 3.

[20] *Ibid.* XII, 15, 25.

[21] *Ibid.* XXI, 14.

[22] *De civitate Dei* XIX, 1, 3, trans. D. B. Zema and G. G. Walsh in *Writings of St. Augustine,* Fathers of the Church (New York: CIMA Publishing Co., 1950), VIII. This series is henceforth designated FOC.

[23] *Contra Faustum Manichaeum* XXII, 52; *De Consensu Evangelistarum* I, 5, 8.

[24] Only the man who has wisdom can be happy. See *De libero arbitrio* II, 13, 36.

[25] *De spiritu et littera* 18; *De Trin.* XII, 14, 22.

[26] *De Trin.* XV, 12, 21.

[27] *Epistolae* 120, 11.

[28] *De Trin.* XII, 2, 2. Augustine's use of "perception" is much broader than its current use, and he does not restrict it to sense perception.

[29] That is, it is peculiar to man as opposed to the brutes. Of course, angels are capable of intellection.

[30] Haddan, in his rendering of *De Trinitate,* translates *cogitatio* as "conception." This is misleading because *cogitatio* has little to do with concepts or classes of things. Gilson translates it as "thought" or "thinking" *(Christian Philosophy,* 75). "Cogitation" is used here because it is free of the connotations of the other translations.

[31] *De Gen. ad Litt.* XII, 7, 16.

[32] *Ibid.* XII, 9, 20.

[33] *Ibid.* XII, 10, 21.

[34] *Ibid.* XII, 11, 22.

[35] *De Trin.* XI, 9, 16. The passage is extremely vague and it may seem that this discussion takes extreme liberties in interpretation. The problems involved, as well as a justification for the interpretation, will be discussed later in this study.

[36] *Ibid.,* trans. A. W. Haddan and revised by W. G. T. Shedd in NPNF III.

Chapter Two

[1] *Contra Academicos* II, 9, 22, trans. Denis J. Kavanagh in FOC II.

[2] "Now I wrote three volumes shortly after my conversion, to remove out of my way the objections which lie, as it were, on the very threshold of faith. And assuredly it was necessary at the very outset to remove this utter despair of reaching truth, which seems to be strengthened by the arguments of these philosophers. . . . Now if assent be taken away, faith goes too; for without assent there can be no belief. And there are truths, whether we know them or not, which must be believed, if we would attain to a happy life, that is, to eternal life." *Enchiridion* 20, trans. J. F. Shaw in NPNF III.

[3] III, 16.

[4] *Ibid.,* III, 1, 1.

[5] *De Beata Vita,* though begun after *Contra Academicos,* was completed

first and thus stands as Augustine's first finished writing after his conversion.

⁶ *Con. Academ.* II, 5, 11.

⁷ Cicero, *Academica* 2, 19, 61; 2, 8, 25.

⁸ *Con. Academ.* II, 5, 12.

⁹ *Ibid.,* II, 7, 20.

¹⁰ *Ibid.,* II, 8, 21.

¹¹ *Ibid.,* III, 9, 19.

¹² *Ibid.,* III, 9, 21.

¹³ *De vera religione* 39, 73, trans. John H. S. Burleigh in *Augustine's Earlier Writings,* The Library of Christian Classics (Philadelphia: Westminster Press, 1953), VI. Henceforth, this work will be designated as AEW.

¹⁴ *Con. Academ.* III, 10, 22.

¹⁵ Unfortunately, Augustine does not consider the most serious difficulty that can be raised in this connection, that since the senses deceive occasionally, how can we know when they do not?

¹⁶ *Con. Academ.* III, 17, 37-39.

¹⁷ *Ibid.,* III, 11, 26.

¹⁸ Of course, this still avoids the problem of deciding how to tell when the senses are reliable.

¹⁹ *De civitate Dei* XIX, 18, trans. M. Dods in NPNF. This remark about the importance of the senses applies only to *scientia. Sapientia* depends upon intellection.

²⁰ *Con. Academ.* III, 11, 26.

²¹ *De vera religione* 33, 62; see also 36, 67.

²² "If we know nothing, and if nothing even appears to us as true, then the entire reason for our dispute will vanish. And if you maintain that what appears to me is not a world, then you are disputing about words only, for I have said that I call it a world." *Con. Academ.* III, 11, 24.

²³ *Ibid.,* III, 11, 25.

²⁴ Augustine is now using the term "world" in a different sense. In this context the term refers to that which appears to the man who is awake and sane.

²⁵ "My only assertion is that this entire mass and frame of bodies in which we exist is either a unit or not a unit, and that it is what it is, whether we be asleep or awake, deranged or of sound mind. Point out how this notion can be false. . . . it must be true that the world is what it is." *Ibid.*

²⁶ *Ibid.*

²⁷ E.g., "The same soul cannot both die and be immortal. A man cannot be at the same time happy and miserable." *Ibid.,* III, 13, 39.

²⁸ E.g., "At the present moment we are either asleep or awake. What I think I see, either is or is not a body." *Ibid.* See also III, 10, 23.

²⁹ *Ibid.*

³⁰ *Ibid.,* III, 11, 25.

³¹ *De civ. Dei* XI, 26. A similar argument can be found in *De Beata Vita* II, 2, 7 and *Soliloquies* II, 1.

³² *Sol.* I, 15, 27. Augustine never explains exactly what he means by "true things." It seems safe to say that he means at least true propositions. Thus, when he says that true things may cease to exist, he can be understood to mean that true propositions can become false.

33 *De ordine* II, 19, 50, trans. R. P. Russell in FOC I.

34 *Sol.* I, 15, 28.

35 William P. Alston and George Nakhnikian, eds., *Readings in Twentieth Century Philosophy* (New York: Free Press, 1963), 7. These examples should not be taken as implying that Augustine held to a correspondence theory of truth. They are offered only as illustrations of the way in which truth remains eternal even though true things (in these instances, true propositions) cease to be true.

36 *Sol.* II, 2, 2, trans. C. C. Starbuck in NPNF.

37 *De vera religione* 30, 56.

38 *De libero arbitrio* II, 12, 34.

39 *Sol.* I, 15, 29.

40 *Confessions* X, 24, trans. J. Pilkington in NPNF. Consider also *De lib. arb.* II, 15, 39, where Augustine writes, "If there is anything more excellent than wisdom, doubtless it, rather is God. But if there is nothing more excellent, then truth itself is God." Trans. John H. S. Burleigh in AEW.

41 *De libero arbitrio* II, 12, 33.

42 See the *Republic* 508-509, 517.

43 This statement is not intended to mean that Augustine's identification of God with the form of good is incorrect. The identification of Plato's God is one of the enduring problems of ancient philosophy. The demiurge of the *Timaeus* was the efficient cause of the world. However, the form of the good was, in a sense, a final cause and Plato's absolute being. Given a choice between the demiurge and the form of the good, Plato's God may very well have been the latter.

Chapter Three

1 *De Trinitate* IX, 1, 1.

2 *De symbolo ad catechumenos* 4, trans. C. L. Cornish in NPNF III.

3 *In Joannis Evangelium* XXVII, 9, trans. Erich Przywara in *An Augustinian Synthesis* (New York: Sheed and Ward, 1945), 58.

4 "Unless ye believe, ye shall not understand." *De libero arbitrio* I, 2, 4.

5 *De utilitate credendi* 2, trans. C. L. Cornish in NPNF III.

6 *Ibid.*, 22.

7 *Ibid.*, 25.

8 *De duabus animabus* 9, 11; *De Trin.* VIII, 4, 6.

9 *De util. cred.* 30.

10 *Ibid.*, 26; *Epistolae* 147, 5; *Confessions* VI, 5.

11 *Epist.* 147, 5; *De ordine* II, 9, 26.

12 *De fide rerum quae non videntur* 2, trans. C. L. Cornish in NPNF III.

13 *Ibid.*

14 *Contra Faustum Manichaeum* XXXII, 19, trans. Richard Stothert in NPNF IV.

15 *Ibid.*, italics added.

16 *Ibid.*

17 *Epist.* 147, 8, trans. Wilfred Parsons in FOC XI.

18 "Faith and Reason in the Thought of St. Augustine" (unpublished Ph.D. dissertation, Syracuse University, 1959), chap. 1.

19 "Of the things which we have seen or now see, we are our own witnesses, but in those which we believe, we are led to our assent by the

testimony of others, because, of the things which we do not recall having seen, or do not now see, we receive indications, either by spoken or written words, or by certain documents, and, when these have been seen, the unseen things are believed. Not without reason do we say that we know not only what we have seen or see, but also what we believe." *Epist.* 147, 8.

20 *Epist.* 102, 38.

21 *De spiritu et littera* 54, trans. Przywara, *Augustinian Synthesis*, 56.

22 *De praedestinatione sanctorum* 5, trans. R. E. Wallis in *BWOA* I.

23 (1) Faith as indirect knowledge; (2) faith as presupposition or assumption; (3) faith as assent to statements as true.

24 It now becomes apparent that even "reason" is used with different meanings. "Reason" no longer designates direct knowledge.

25 *Sermons* 43, 7.

26 *Serm.* 43, 3-4. However, Augustine qualifies this when he considers faith's relation to *sapientia*. In the case of some Christian doctrines we must believe what we do not yet understand.

27 *De vera religione* 24, 45; 25, 46. Compare also: "For who cannot see that thinking is prior to believing? For no one believes anything unless he has first thought that it is to be believed." *De praed. Sanct.* 5.

28 *Epist.* 147, 2, 7.

29 *De civitate Dei* XXII, 29.

30 Augustine emphasized judgment instead of proposition. However, the term "proposition" is a modern synonym. Even though Augustine did not speak of propositions, he did believe that revelation is a communication of truth that can be expressed in meaningful sentences. My argument is not necessarily a criticism of what might be termed a noncognitive view of revelation, but it is argued that such a position cannot be attributed to St. Augustine.

31 Alan Richardson, *Christian Apologetics* (New York: Harper, 1947), 238.

32 *Epist.* 82, 3 and 5.

33 *De lib. arb.* I, 2, 4.

34 *De diversis quaestionibus*, qu. 48.

35 *Enarratio in Psalmum* 118, 18, 3, trans. Praywara, *Augustinian Synthesis*, 59.

36 *Epist.* 120, 1, 3. In this sense faith helps us understand greater things. "For although, unless he understands somewhat, no man can believe in God, nevertheless by the very faith whereby he believes, he is helped to the understanding of great things *(ampliora)*." *Enarr. in Ps.* 118, 18, 3, trans. Przywara, *Augustinian Synthesis*, 59.

37 *Contra Academicos* II, 3, 8.

38 *De moribus ecclesiae Catholicae* I, 17, 31, trans. Richard Stothert in *NPNF* IV. See also *De util. cred.* 16, 34.

39 "Faith and Reason," *A Companion to the Study of St. Augustine* (New York: Oxford University Press, 1955), 289ff.

40 *Ibid.*, 310.

41 Aristotle, *De anima* III, 8, 423b 28f, trans. J. A. Smith in *Basic Works of Aristotle*, ed. Richard McKeon (New York: Random House, 1941).

42 An excellent discussion of this aspect of Augustine's thought is to be found in Gordon Lewis' "Faith and Reason in the Thought of St. Augustine." Lewis makes clear that for Augustine man's reason cannot function in isolation from his entire nature. "An exercise of will, such as

faith, is not, for Augustine, an arbitrary performance unrelated to the rational side of man's nature. The will and the reason are one essence. Neither may be given priority exclusive of the other." Lewis, 78f; see *In Joan. Evang.* XXVI, 4.

43 *De Trin.* IX, 12, 18.

44 "We must therefore in your case try not to make you understand divine things, which is impossible, but to make you desire to understand." *De mor. eccl. Cath.* 17, 31; see also *De util. cred.* 29 and *De beata vita* 14.

45 John 7:17.

46 *De Trin.* X, 11, 17.

47 *De fide et symbolo* 10, 19, trans. S. D. F. Salmond in NPNF III. This is a profound psychological truth. Whatever our natural ability to know and learn, it can be made ineffectual by a lack of interest.

48 *Epist.* 55, 10, 18.

49 *Conf.* XIII, 9; see also *Epist.* 118, 5 and *De civ. Dei* XI, 3.

50 *Epist.* 118, 5, trans. Wilfred Parsons in FOC X.

51 *De lib. arb.* III, 18, 52.

52 *Ibid.,* III, 22, 64.

53 *De agone Christiano* XIII, 14, trans. Robert B. Russell in FOC IV.

54 *De lib. arb.* III, 22, 65.

55 *De ordine* II, 19, 51, trans. Robert P. Russell in FOC I and *De doctrina Christiana* I, 10, 10, trans. John Gavigan in FOC IV. See also *Sol.* I, 6, 12; *Enarr. in Ps.* 44, 25; 118, 18, 3; *De Trin.* I, 1, 3.

56 The word "thought" is important here because even though many believe things unworthy of belief, no one believes that which he thinks is false or unworthy of belief.

57 Indirect knowledge.

58 This example should not be taken to mean that all who might be regarded as "naturalists" hold their views uncritically.

Chapter Four

1 *De Genesi ad Litteram* XII, 24, 51.

2 *Ennead* IV, 2, 1.

3 *Ennead* IV, 3, 26, trans. Stephen Mackenna in *Plotinus on the Nature of the Soul* (London: Medici Society, 1924).

4 *De Trinitate* XV, 7, 11. Augustine's understanding of this point is in the Platonic tradition but, as usual, what he learns from others is modified in the light of the Scriptures. He refuses to follow Plato and the Manicheans in holding the body to be evil. If the body were really intrinsically evil, he asks, why would God resurrect the body? *(De civitate Dei* XIII, 16) Another modification of Platonism is Augustine's greater emphasis on the unity of man. While man's body and soul are both substances, man also is a substance *(De Trin.* XV, 7, 11). It may be that Augustine never succeeded in harmonizing the Platonic dualism with the Scriptural emphasis on the unity of man, but he tried.

5 *De Trin.* XV, 7, 11.

6 *De quantitate animae* XIII, 22.

7 Vernon J. Bourke, *Augustine's Quest of Wisdom* (Milwaukee: Bruce Publishing Co., 1945), 112.

8 *De quant. animae* 23.

9 *De Gen. ad Litt.* XII, 24.

10 By "Platonists" Augustine means such Neoplatonists as Plotinus. Augustine appears to have had little acquaintance with the actual writings of Plato.

11 *De civ. Dei* VIII, 7.

12 *Ibid.*

13 *De ordine* II, 2, 5. The words are spoken by Trygetius, but the context makes it clear that Augustine concurs.

14 "None of the things which a bodily sense reveals to us can remain unchanged for even an instant, and that everything shifts, flows away, and has no hold on the present, which is to say, in Latin, that it has no being." *Epistolae* 2.

15 *De quant. animae* 30, 58, trans. John J. McMahon in FOC II.

16 *Ibid.*, 25, 49.

17 *Ibid.*, 26, 50.

18 *Ibid.*

19 *Ibid.*, 26, 51.

20 *Ibid.*, 27, 53.

21 *Ibid.*, 28, 54.

22 *Ibid.*

23 *De Trin.* XV, 12, 21.

24 *Ennead* IV, 6, 1.

25 *Ibid.*, IV, 5, 3.

26 *Ibid.*, IV, 6, 1.

27 *Ibid.*

28 *De Gen. ad Litt.* XII, 16, 33.

29 *De Trin.* XI, 2, 2. Compare this to *Theatetus* 184 cd, where Plato regards the senses as instruments through which the soul perceives.

30 *De Trin.* XI, 2, 2-5.

31 *De quant. animae* 23, 41.

32 *De musica* VI, 5, 10, trans. Robert C. Taliaferro in FOC II.

33 *Ibid.*, VI, 4, 7.

34 *Ibid.*, VI, 5, 8.

35 *Ibid.*, Italics added.

36 *Ennead* IV, 5, 1.

37 *Ibid.*

38 *Ibid.*, IV, 5, 3.

39 *Ibid.*, VI, 9, 8.

40 Written about A.D. 388.

41 *De quant. animae* 23, 43.

42 *Ibid.*

43 *De musica*, begun in 387 and completed in A.D. 391.

44 *De musica* VI, 5.

45 See *Epist.* 7.

46 *Epist.* 137, 2, 5. Written in A.D. 412.

47 He admits his uncertainty about the sense of smell but does not consider it.

48 *Ibid.*

49 *Ibid.*

50 *Ibid.*

51 *De ordine* II, 11, 30.

52 *De immortalitate animae* 15, 24, trans. Ludwig Schopp in FOC I.

[53] *Retractationum* I, 11, 4, cited and trans. R. P. Russell in FOC I, 308n.

[54] See Etienne Gilson, *The Christian Philosophy of Saint Augustine* (New York: Random House, 1960), 347f.

[55] *Epist.* 137, 2, 6.

[56] *Ibid.*

[57] *Ennead* III, 6, 3.

[58] *Ibid.*, I, 1, 6.

[59] *Ibid.*, IV, 4, 23.

[60] *Ibid.*, IV, 3, 26.

[61] *Ibid.*, IV, 3, 23.

[62] *Ibid.*, IV, 7, 8.

[63] *Ibid.*, IV, 4, 25.

[64] *Ibid.*, IV, 4, 23.

[65] Gordon Clark, "Plotinus' Theory of Sensation," *Philosophical Review*, LI (July 1942), 375.

[66] See *Epist.* 6.

[67] *Epist.* 7.

[68] *De Trin.* XI, 2, 5.

[69] *De Trin.* XI, 2, 3; see also *De Civ. Dei* VIII, 5 where he writes, "Now, whatever can be so imagined in the mind's eye is certainly not a body but only a likeness of a body."

[70] *Epist.* 147, 38.

[71] "When we speak of bodies by means of the bodily sense, there arises in our mind some likeness of them, which is a phantasm of the memory; for the bodies themselves are not at all in the mind, when we think them, but only the likeness of these bodies." *De Trin.* IX, 11, 16.

[72] "Then whatever this memory contains from the motions of the mind brought to bear on the passions of the body are called *phantasiae* in Greek." *De musica* VI, 11, 32.

[73] *De musica* VI, 11, 32. Also of importance in this connection is *Epist.* 7, where phantasms are said to be nothing but "likenesses of corporeal things in the memory." See also *De vera religione* X, 18 and *De Trin.* XI, 5, 8.

[74] *Epist.* 7.

[75] Descartes, *Meditation* III, trans. Norman Kemp Smith in *Descartes' Philosophical Writings* (New York: Modern Library Edition, 1958), 197.

[76] *Epist.* 7.

[77] *De Trin.* IX, 6, 10; VIII, 6, 9.

[78] *Epist.* 7.

[79] *Ibid.*

[80] *Ibid.*

[81] "The Active Theory of Sensation in St. Augustine," *The New Scholasticism*, XXX (April 1956), 167f.

[81] See Bourke, *Augustine's Quest*, 113.

[83] Frederick Copleston, *A History of Philosophy*, II: *Augustine to Scotus* (Westminster, Md.: The Newman Press, 1962), 56. Augustine's position on the question of perception is clearly realistic, *i.e.*, sensible objects exist independently of their being perceived. However, it is not too well known that in one of his earliest philosophical writings, the *Soliloquies*, Augustine did consider a form of idealism remarkably similar to that of the eighteenth-century British idealist George Berkeley. See *Soliloquies* II, 7.

Chapter Five

[1] *De Trinitate* XII, 1, 1-2.
[2] *De Trin.* IX, 6, 10.
[3] *De quantitate animae* 33, 70-76.
[4] I follow Bourke's translation here rather than the usual but less meaningful rendering, "art." See Vernon J. Bourke, *Augustine's Quest of Wisdom* (Milwaukee: Bruce Publishing Co., 1945), 102.
[5] *De quant. animae* 33, 70.
[6] *Ibid.*, 33, 71.
[7] *Ibid.*, 33, 72.
[8] *De Trin.* IX, 12, 18.
[9] *Confessions* X, 11.
[10] *De Trin.* XIV, 6, 8. It should be remembered that the Haddan translation of *De Trin.* designates *cogitatio* by the misleading term "conception."
[11] *Ibid.* XI, 9, 16.
[12] *De immortalitate animae* 3, 3; 7, 12.
[13] This explains how the Bible can speak of both men and beasts as "living souls." See Gen. 1:24 and 2:7.
[14] Augustine borrows the term from the philosopher Varro (*De civitate Dei* VII, 23), but the distinction between *animus* (mind) and *anima* (soul) was probably first introduced into Latin by Lucretius.
[15] *De civitate Dei* XI, 3.
[16] There are times, however, when Augustine uses *animus* and *anima* with no apparent difference in meaning. See *De quant. animae* 13, 22.
[17] *De Trin.* XIV, 16, 22.
[18] *De anima et ejus origine* II, 2, 2.
[19] *De fide et symbolo* 10, 23, trans. S. D. F. Salmond in NPNF III.
[20] *De Trin.* XIV, 16,22.
[21] *Ibid.* Augustine apparently borrowed this usage from Porphyry. See *De civ. Dei* X, 9.
[22] *De Genesi ad Litteram* XII, 9, 20.
[23] *De Trin.* XV, 1, 1. See also *De fide et symbolo* 4, 8 where he writes, "Man is in nothing separated from the cattle but in (the possession of) a rational spirit, which is also named mind *(mens)*." Also in this connection, see *De libero arbitrio* I, 8, 18.
[24] *De vera religione* 29, 53.
[25] *Ibid.*, 30, 55.
[26] *De civ. Dei* XI, 2.
[27] *De lib. arb.* I, 9, 19.
[28] *De ordine* II, 11, 30.
[29] *Soliloquiorum* I, 6, 13; see also *De immort. animae* 6, 10.
[30] *De immort. animae* 6, 10.
[31] "See whether you think that in a youth, or a man, or (to remove any ground for doubt) anyone capable of thinking, provided he has a sound mind, reason is inherent, in the same way that health is inherent in the body as long as it is free of disease and wounds." *De quant. animae* 27, 52.
[32] "The process of being led on to something unknown from premises that are granted or evident is not reason itself. This process is not always present in the sound mind, but reason is." *Ibid.*
[33] *Ibid.*

³⁴ *De Trin.* XII, 2, 2, does not contradict this statement, as the "higher reason" mentioned is contrasted not with the lower reason but with sense perception in the brutes. All the passage teaches is that man can judge corporeal things in the light of eternal standards because he possesses a reason. It should not be understood to mean that the *superior ratio* is the faculty that so judges sensible things.

³⁵ *In Joannis Evangelium* XV, 19-20, trans. John Gibb and James Innes in NPNF VII.

³⁶ Augustine uses *intellectus* and *ratio* at times to refer to the same function of the soul and at other times to different functions, suggesting that he never attempted to systematize his thought on this subject.

³⁷ *Epistolae* 147, 18, 45.

³⁸ *De Trin.* XI, 3, 6.

³⁹ "In Augustinism, thought *(cogitatio)* is merely the movement by which the soul gathers, assembles and collects all the hidden knowledge it possesses and has not yet discovered, in order to be able to fix its gaze upon it. Really, therefore, thinking, learning and remembering are all one to the soul." Etienne Gilson, *The Christian Philosophy of Saint Augustine* (New York: Random House, 1960), 75.

⁴⁰ *Confessions* X, 8; *De Trin.* VIII, 6; *De civ. Dei* XI, 26.

⁴¹ *Conf.* X, 8.

⁴² *Ibid.,* X, 13.

⁴³ *Ibid.,* X, 8.

⁴⁴ *De Trin.* XII, 2, 2.

⁴⁵ *Ibid.*

⁴⁶ *Christian Philosophy,* 110f.

⁴⁷ *Conf.* X, 12.

⁴⁸ However, Kant's *a priori* is an empty form and Augustine's has content. See also *De Trin.* XIV, 7, 9 and *Conf.* X, 17-20.

⁴⁹ *De Trin.* XII, 14, 23.

⁵⁰ *Conf.* X, 9.

⁵¹ *De Trin.* XIV, 7, 9.

⁵² *Ibid.*

⁵³ *Conf.* X, 17-20.

⁵⁴ *Ibid.,* X, 17.

⁵⁵ *Ibid.*

⁵⁶ *Ibid.,* X, 20.

⁵⁷ *Ibid.,* X, 21.

⁵⁸ *Ibid.*

⁵⁹ *Ibid.*

⁶⁰ *De lib. arb.* II, 3, 9.

⁶¹ *Ibid.,* II, 3, 8.

⁶² *Ibid.*

⁶³ *Ibid.,* II, 3, 9.

⁶⁴ *Ibid.,* I, 6, 13.

⁶⁵ *De Trin.* XI, 2.

⁶⁶ *De Trin.* XI, 3.

⁶⁷ *Ibid.,* XI, 3, 6.

⁶⁸ *Ibid.,* XI, 8, 15.

⁶⁹ *De quant. animae* 27, 52.

⁷⁰ Much confusion will result if it is not understood what Augustine

means by species. The problem is complicated by the fact that he uses species synonymously with *ideae* and *formae* (see *De div. quaest.* 46, 1-2). If species is used with this meaning in *De Trin.* XI, 9, 16, then this passage teaches that for Augustine sensation in some way imprints the universal upon the sense organ, and this universal is passed along to the memory and becomes the basis of cognition. Needless to say, this was not Augustine's view. Instead, it must be understood that when he uses species in this context, he is using it with the meaning it ordinarily had in Latin—sight or appearance. So when he talks about the species of a physical object, he must be understood to mean the appearance of that object. That this is his meaning of species can be seen by considering *De Trin.* XI, 2, 3. "And therefore we cannot, indeed, say that a visible thing produces the sense; yet it (the visible thing) produces the form (species), which is, as it were, its own likeness, which comes to be in the sense, when we perceive anything by seeing." This passage definitely equates species with the likeness of a thing. See also *De Trin.* XI, 2, 4.

71 *De Trin.* XI, 2, 3.

72 This statement seems inconsistent with Augustine's active theory of sensation. It must be remembered, however, that it is the soul that is active in sensation. The sense organ plays a passive role in receiving impressions from sensible objects.

Chapter Six

1 See Lawrence F. Jansen, "The Divine Ideas in the Writings of St. Augustine," *The Modern Schoolman*, XXII (1945), 117-31.

2 *De doctrina Christiana* II, 32, 50, trans. John J. Gavigan in FOC IV.

3 *De vera religione* 30, 55, trans. John H. S. Burleigh in AEW.

4 *De libero arbitrio* II, 8, 20, trans. John H. S. Burleigh in AEW.

5 *Ibid.* II, 8, 21.

6 *Ibid.*, II, 8, 22.

7 *Ibid.*

8 *Ibid.*, II, 8, 23.

9 *Ibid.*

10 *Soliloquies* I, 9, trans. C. C. Starbuck in BWOA I.

11 *De lib. arb.* II, 10, 28. He claims similar status for the principles of beauty in *De lib. arb.* II, 16, 41.

12 *De doct. Christ.* II, 38, 56; *De lib. arb.* II, 8, 20.

13 *Phaedo* 72D- 76A; *Meno* 85C- 86D.

14 For example, "For while in your view the soul has brought no art with it, in mine, on the other hand, it has brought every art; for to learn is nothing else than to recall and remember." *De quantitate animae* 20, 34.

15 *De Trinitate* XIV, 11, 14.

16 *Retractionum* I, 8, trans. McMahon in FOC II, 97n. See also *Retract.* I, 4.

17 *De Trin.* XII, 15, 24.

18 *Ibid.* There is some question about the relevance of Augustine's objection. His remarks might apply to Plato's position in the *Meno*, but Plato's view as set forth in the *Phaedo* would avoid the objection, because in the latter work Plato teaches that the forms were observed not in a former life (*i.e.*, life in the body) but during man's existence between

death and reincarnation. Augustine's point that there are few geometricians would then be irrelevant, as geometrical knowledge would result from the soul's vision of the forms while freed from the body.

19 *Retract.* I, 4, trans. John H. S. Burleigh in AEW, 18.

20 *De magistro* IV, 8.

21 *Ibid.*, II, 3; III.

22 *Ibid.*, VII, trans. G. C. Leckie in BWOA I.

23 "Then the difference between noun and word is the same as the difference between horse and animal." *Ibid.*, IV.

24 *Ibid.*, V. In Part I of his *Philosophical Investigations* (New York: Macmillan, 1953), Ludwig Wittgenstein wrote a famous but unfair critique of Augustine's philosophy of language. According to Wittgenstein, Augustine taught that language consists only of words which name or refer to something; that is, every word has a meaning and this meaning is that to which the word refers. Augustine is also supposed to have taught that the meanings of words are learned by ostensive definition, for example, we teach a child the meaning of a word by pointing to its referent. In *De magistro* V, Augustine clearly recognizes that some words perform functions other than naming. Wittgenstein's case is also weakened by the text quoted in f.n. 23. If names are a species of *verbum* (symbols), then there are words which do not name.

25 *Ibid.*, VII.

26 Augustine makes this point in chapter five of *De magistro* using a different example.

27 *Ibid.*, VII.

28 *Ibid.*, III.

29 "Not even a wall can be shown without a sign, as far as I can see from our discussion at this point. For the directing of the finger is certainly not the wall, but through it a sign is given by which the wall may be seen. I see nothing, therefore, which can be shown without signs." *Ibid.*

30 *Ibid.* The argument that follows is interesting for two reasons. First, it can be used to refute Wittgenstein's charge that Augustine held that one can only learn the meaning of a word by having someone point to its referent. As Augustine demonstrates, it is impossible to define the word "walk" by example. Second, the very argument Augustine uses to establish his point anticipates one of Wittgenstein's most distinctive methods of argumentation.

31 *Ibid.*, XIII. This argument of course is invalid. The words "teach" and "understand" are used equivocally.

32 *Ibid.*

33 *Ibid.*

34 *Ibid.*

35 *Ibid.*, X.

36 *Ibid.*, XI.

37 *Ibid.*

38 *Ibid.*, XII.

39 John 1:9

40 *Ibid.*, XI, trans. John H. S. Burleigh in AEW.

41 *De Trin.* XII, 15, 24.

42 *De ordine* II, 3, 10; *Sol.* I, 6, 12.

43 *Sol.* I, 1, 3.

[44] *Sol.* I, 8, 15, trans. John H. S. Burleigh in *AEW*.
[45] *Epistolae* 120, 10, trans. Wifred Parsons in FOC.

Chapter Seven

[1] Found in *De anima* 3, 5, 430a, 17ff.
[2] *Summa Theogica* I, 1. 84, a. 6.
[3] *Truth*, XI, 3, reply, trans. James V. McGlynn (Chicago: Regnery, 1953), II, 95.
[4] His position is set forth in *Saint Augustin* (Paris: Gabalda, 1932) and "La philosophie augustinienne ignore-t-elle l'abstraction?" in *Nouvelle Revue Theologique* (1930), 1-14.
[5] Charles Boyer, *L'idée de vérité dans la philosophie de s. Augustin* (Paris, 1921), 206. Cited and trans. by M. C. D'Arcy in "The Philosophy of St. Augustine" in *A Monument to St. Augustine*, ed. D'Arcy (London: Sheed and Ward, 1945), 180f.
[6] *De Trinitate* XII, 15, 24, italics added.
[7] See *De spiritualibus creaturis* X.
[8] See *The Christian Philosophy of Saint Augustine* (New York: Random House, 1960), 290.
[9] For example, see Frederick Copleston, *A History of Philosophy*, II: *Augustine to Scotus* (Westminster, Md.: The Newman Press, 1962), 389.
[10] C. E. Scheutzinger, *The German Controversy on Saint Augustine's Illumination Theory* (New York: Pageant Press, 1960), 44.
[11] (Paris, 1902), I, 2268-2472. This work has recently been republished as *A Guide to the Thought of St. Augustine*, trans. Ralph Bastian (Chicago: Regnery, 1960).
[12] *Thought of Augustine*, 113.
[13] The view that these concepts are innate is advanced by Richard K. Ackworth in "God and Human Knowledge," *The Downside Review*, LXXV (1957) 207-14.
[14] Copleston, *Augustine to Scotus*, 64.
[15] Introduction to Portalié's *Thought of Augustine*, xxx.
[16] *History of Medieval Philosophy*, 3d ed. (New York: Longman, Green and Co., 1909), 95.
[17] *Die Erkenntnislehre des hl. Augustinus* (Sarnen, 1920).
[18] Gilson, *Christian Philosophy*, 79, 86, 91.
[19] Copleston, *Augustine to Scotus*, 65.
[20] Support for this point was contained in an argument noted earlier. Copleston cannot explain in a way consistent with Augustine's remarks in *De libero arbitrio* how man attains a knowledge of unity. The notion of unity cannot possibly be derived from experience. In order for Copleston to maintain his thesis he would have to ignore these texts and assert that somehow man abstracts the notion of unity from particulars. This is not Augustine.
[21] Gilson, *Christian Philosophy*, 297.
[22] *Ibid.*, 84.

Chapter Eight

[1] The word "Thomist" is now being used in a broader sense than before. Previously, it referred to advocates of the so-called Thomist interpretation

of Augustine's illumination theory. It now applies to even Copleston and Gilson, who reject the Thomist interpretation.

2 Nicolas Malebranche, *De la recherche de la vérité*, 3, 2, 6.

3 *Ibid.* Malebranche knew better than to claim Augustine's support for this aspect of his thought.

4 *De ordine* II, 8, 25.

5 *De Trinitate* XIV, 15, 21.

6 *De Trin.* II, 6, 11.

7 *De libero arbitrio* II, 15, 39.

8 *De Trin.* XII, 2, 2.

9 *Confessions* X, 12.

10 *De immortalitate animae* 4, trans. Ludwig Schopp in FOC II.

11 *Ibid.*, 6.

12 *De Trin.* VIII, 3, 4.

13 *De civitate Dei* VIII, 6, italics added.

14 *Ibid.*

15 *Ibid.*

16 See *De diversis quaestionibus* 46.

17 *De civ. Dei* VIII, 6.

18 "In every changeable thing, the form which makes it that which it is, whatever be its mode or nature, can only *be* through Him who truly *is*, because He is unchangeable." *Ibid.*

19 *In Joannis Evangelium* III, 4, in NPNF VII.

20 XX, 7.

21 *Contra Faustum Manichaeum* XX, 7, trans. Richard Stothert in NPNF IV, italics added.

22 *De immort. animae* 4.

23 *De lib. arb.* II, 16, 41.

24 *De Trin.* VIII, 3, 4.

25 Portalié, *A Guide to the Thought of St. Augustine* (Chicago: Regnery, 1960), 111.

26 "God and Human Knowledge," *The Downside Review*, LXXV (1957), 108f.

27 *De Gestis Pelagii* 3, 7.

28 *De Genesi ad Litteram* XII, 31, 59, cited by Gilson, *The Christian Philosophy of Saint Augustine* (New York: Random House, 1960), 93.

29 B. B. Warfield, *Calvin and Augustine* (Philadelphia: Presbyterian and Reformed Publishing Co., 1956), 397.

30 Gilson, *Christian Philosophy*, 78.

31 See Frederick Copleston, *A History of Philosophy*, II: *Augustine to Scotus* (Westminster, Md.: The Newman Press, 1962), 64f.

32 *Ibid.*, 93f.

33 Gilson does use the argument with care and discrimination. He does not hesitate to point out texts implying ontologism that do not refer to a mystical experience. See Gilson, *Christian Philosophy*, 95.

34 *Ibid.*, 91.

35 *Confessions* VII, 17.

36 Augustine is alluding to God's words to Moses in Exod. 3:14 in which He reveals His name as "I AM THAT I AM." This name has usually been taken to mean that God is the eternally present one.

37 Gilson, *Christian Philosophy*, 96.

38 *De lib. arb.* II, 3, 7 to II, 6, 14.

39 *De Trin.* VIII, 3, 4-5.

40 *Ibid.*, VIII, 3, 4.

41 *Ibid.*, VIII, 3, 5. I have capitalized references to God.

42 *De civ. Dei* XI, 2.

43 William James, *The Varieties of Religious Experience* (London: Longmans, Green and Co., 1902), 371.

44 Compare: " 'Contemplation' is the word that will be met with in St. Augustine, St. Gregory, and St. Bernard to designate what is now commonly called 'the mystical experience.' " Dom Cuthbert Butler, *Western Mysticism* (New York: Dutton and Co., 1923), 3.

45 "Dividum et incommutabile aliquid discritur," *Con. Faust. Man.* XII, 54.

46 *De Trin.* IX, 7, 12.

47 *Conf.* XII, 25.

48 Johannes Hessen, *Augustine Metaphysik der Erkenntnis* (Berlin, 1931), 211.

49 Gilson, *Christian Philosophy*, 92, 94.

50 *Ibid.*, 94.

51 See Rom. 1:18-25.

52 *De Trin.* XII, 14, 23.

53 *Ibid.*, XIV, 15, 21.

54 Gilson, *Christian Philosophy*, 91.

55 *Ibid.*, 92.

56 For example, *De lib. arb.* II, 10, 29 and *De Trin.* XIV, 15, 21.

57 *De lib. arb.* II, 8, 20-22; II, 9, 26.

58 Gilson, *Christian Philosophy*, 297 n.

59 *De Trin.* IX, 6, 9.

60 *Ibid.*, IX, 6, 11.

61 *De Trin.* XII, 15, 24.

62 Gilson, *Christian Philosophy*, 95.

63 *Ibid.*, 82.

64 *De Trin.* IX, 11, 16.

65 1 Cor. 13:12.

66 *De Trin.* VIII, 9, 13.

67 Gilson, *Christian Philosophy*, 110f.

68 *Ibid.*

69 This discussion follows a suggestion by Warfield, *Calvin and Augustine.*

70 *Ibid.* 402.

71 Armand Maurer, *Medieval Philosophy* (New York: Random House, 1962), 218.

index

Abstraction, notion of, 96, 100
Academicians. *See* Skepticism
Ackworth, Richard, 110, 139n13
Agent intellect, 95, 97
Agnitio, 33, 34
Anima. *See* Animus
Animals: sensation in, 41, 42, 128n29; compared to man, 60, 63
Animatio, 61
Animus, 63, 135n14, 135n16
A priori forms of thought, 68, 69, 78, 90, 109, 110, 136n48
Aquinas, St. Thomas: þifurcation of philosophy and theology, 1; closed system of philosophy, 2; interpretation of Augustine's illumination theory, 94-97
Aristotle: closed system of philosophy, 2; passive theory of sensation, 43, 46; three levels of soul, 61; doctrine of active intellect, 94
Authority. *See* Faith

Bacon, Roger, 97
Beatitude. *See* Happiness
Berkeley, George, 59, 134n83
Bible: and deceptiveness of senses, 16; and faith, 26, 27, 29, 31; authority of, 32; and propositional revelation, 31-33
Body. *See* Sense organ, Sense perception, and Soul
Bonaventure, St., 97
Bourke, Vernon J., 40, 98, 135n4
Boyer, Father Charles, 95

Christ, Jesus, 84, 90, 91, 92
Cicero, 13

Clark, Gordon H., 53
Cogitation: role in knowledge, 9, 62, 63, 136n39; relation to spiritual vision, 10; and memory, 66-75 *passim*, 136n39; passage from *sentientis* to *cogitantis*, 72-75; and trinity of inner man, 74, 75; translation of *cogitatio*, 128n30; mentioned, 10, 63
Cognitio, 33, 34
Contemplation, 8, 115, 116, 141n44
Contra Academicos, exposition of, 12-20, 128n5
Copleston, Frederick: problem of external world, 59, 134n83; criticism of Franciscan interpretation, 97, 98; interpretation of Augustine's illumination theory, 99-101; mentioned, 1, 139n20
Cushman, Robert E., 33, 34

De Magistro, exposition of, 84-92
Democritus, 46
De Musica, discussion of Book VI, 45
Descartes, René: on deceptiveness of senses, 15-18; and the *Cogito*, 20; three classes of ideas, 55-58; and solipsism, 59; on mind and body, 103
DeWulf, Maurice, 98
Dialectic, 84, 85
Ding an sich, 77

Epicureans, 40, 43, 46, 88
Ethics, 81, 109

Faith: necessary element of knowledge, 1; relation to reason, 1,

Malebranche, Nicholas, 102, 103, 104, 120, 139n3
Manichaeanism, 3, 24-27, 46
Mathematics, no empirical basis for, 78-81
Memory: its role in knowledge, 10, 11, 66-75 *passim*; provides objection to passive theory of sensation, 43; memory images, 54, 55; and cogitation, 62, 63, 66-75 *passim*; discussion of Augustine's use of, 66-75 *passim*; as storehouse of virtual knowledge, 66, 68, 69, 70; and future experience, 67; and dispositional knowledge, 70; and knowledge of God, 70; and knowledge of blessed life, 70-72; and interior sense, 73; mentioned, 60, 61, 87. *See also Phantasia, Phantasm*
Mens (Mind): relation to *spiritus* and *animus*, 63; superior to senses, 64; relation to divine illumination, 65, 92, 118, 119; the "eye of the mind," 74, 75, 91, 92, 105; a created light, 107, 108
Mysticism, 102, 112-18, 120

Nakhnikian, George, 21
Necessary truth. *See* Truth
Neoplatonism, its influence on Augustine, 3-6 *passim. See also* Plotinus, Platonists

Oates, Whitney, 2, 3
Occasionalism. *See* Malebranche
One, The. *See* Plotinus
Ontologist interpretation of illumination, 102-123 *passim*
Ontology, 4, 5
Outer man, trinity of, 60, 73, 74

Paradoxes in Augustine's epistemology, 104-111
Parmenides, 85
Phantasia, 55, 134n72
Phantasm, 55, 80, 134n71, 134n73
Philo, 7, 127n15, 127n17
Plato: open system of philosophy, 2; allegory of cave, 4, 117; related metaphysics and epistemology, 4; on sensation, 40; on man's knowledge of a priori truth, 69, 90; knowledge as recollection, 69, 82-84 *passim*, 137n18; use of dialectical method, 84; his God, 117, 118, 130n43; view of man, 132n4; mentioned, 96, 133n29

Plato *(continued):*
Platonists, the, 3-6 *passim*, 37, 40, 41, 133n10
Plotinus: influence on Augustine, 4, 5; doctrine of the forms, 7; view of sensation, 39, 40, 43-47; view of soul, 39, 40; theory of sympathy, 47, 50, 51; view of God, 51, 127n16; role of sense organ in sensation, 52, 53; mentioned, 132n4
Porphyry, 135n21
Portalié, E., 97, 110, 111
Probability and skepticism, 13, 14

Ratio hominis, 5, 7
Ratio inferior, 5, 7, 8, 65, 75
Ratio superior, 5, 7, 8, 65, 75
Rationes aeternae: and God, 5, 6, 23, 76, 77, 92, 107, 118; Augustine's definition, 6, 76; archetypes of this world, 6, 7, 77, 106, 107; Philo and Plotinus on, 7; and intellectual vision, 9, 76-93 *passim*, 122; and truth, 22, 122; superior to human mind, 63, 67, 77, 105; and memory, 67, 68, 69, 70; and *scientia*, 76, 109, 122; and *sapientia*, 76; man's knowledge of the forms, 77-93, 94-101, 104-23; not known by senses, 77-81; not known by Platonic recollection, 82-84; not known by teaching, 84-91; in Franciscan interpretation of illumination, 97; three paradoxes concerning, 104-11; in man's mind, 105-10 *passim*, 118, 119; mentioned, 60, 64, 104
Rationes seminales, 6, 51
Ratiocination *(ars)*, 61, 62, 64, 65
Ray theory of sight, 48-50
Reason *(ratio)*: its relation to faith, 1, 24-38 *passim*; noetic effects of